Divo
Reality

A Journey Through the Darkness to Moving On

By
Daniel Lamirande

ISBN 978-1-7380402-1-6

DEDICATION

For Lori, the love of my life and the one who always believes in me.

For Jordan, Aline, Alex, my children.

For Roger and Jeannine, my parents.

For Julie, my sister.

TABLE OF CONTENTS

Preface

When our life suddenly changes due to divorce, it becomes a life-shifting event and seldom results in a small obstacle to overcome. It changes everything. Trying to make sense of it all in one of the darkest moments of our lives can be extremely challenging, not to mention alienating, disconnecting, and isolating.

This book is not anti-marriage or against the concept of marriage itself. It's not about criticizing or being disrespectful regarding our former spouse. It's about us, our divorce, and getting real about it. As the book title Divorced from Reality suggests, when facing divorce, we need to get real about what that means and face reality.

Living in denial has helped no one, ever. Denial is the refusal to accept the reality about our situation, ourselves, and life. At its core, it robs us of our precious limited time. Denial can be destructive by prolonging the inevitable. Its most powerful consequence is its ability to cripple us psychologically and emotionally when we are at our weakest.

We are most susceptible to denial when we feel that reality threatens our perceived sense of control. We believe that by denying our circumstances, we choose to take control of our lives. What we are doing is giving up. Not to put too fine a point on it, but denial is like the drug used by an addict to numb the pain that they feel. It becomes a coping mechanism for past or current hurts. There is a reason why denial is first in the five stages of grief. It offers us the simplest method to deal with a traumatic event: Avoidance.

If this sounds like you, don't feel bad. This is an extremely human response, and everyone has experienced it at some point. The important thing is to recognize it and make plans to overcome it. Sometimes we hold on to the very things that are destroying us. We keep a white-knuckle grip on the things we should be letting go. It's like walking through the darkness. Shining a light on these areas can be very cleansing.

Before we shine a light, however, we must no longer fear the darkness. Many things can hide in darkness, but the light has the power to expose them.

It exposes the truth, and the truth sets us free. We are then empowered to course correct, and we can finally let go.

There is freedom in letting go. Letting go of societal pressures. Letting go of unrealistic expectations. Letting go of the guilt, the shame, and the condemnation. Letting go of what you think your life was supposed to be. There is freedom in accepting who you are, faults and all.

This isn't about admitting that you are not perfect. It's more than that. It's about admitting you are a flawed human being influenced by your environment, family, friends, childhood, and work. As a unique human being, you have seen the world through a different lens than everyone else. You have seen and heard information and processed it according to your experiences.

As you begin your journey to self-discovery, the adage that it takes a village to raise a child is very apt here. You will require wisdom from those who have taken this journey before you.

You will need support from those who bear the same scars, who have fought similar battles, and have succeeded where others have failed.

You will take the knowledge collected from those who have observed and studied human behavior and leverage it to achieve success in your own life on your terms.

However, they cannot take the journey for you. Only you can make that decision and forge your own path. The journey of a thousand miles begins with a single step.

And for this part of the journey, the first mile, you must walk alone.

Daniel Lamirande

Chapter 1
The Wrecking Ball

"Divorce is like an amputation: You survive it, but there's less of you."

– Margaret Atwood

Anyone who has experienced a divorce can relate to the above quote. Divorce is ugly, painful, and can leave us with lifelong scars. No one is ever really prepared for divorce. Young people may dream about getting married one day, but none of them dream about getting divorced. In most cases, we are ill-prepared for marriage, let alone for divorce.

Marriage was supposed to be a once-in-a-lifetime event until death do us part. It was all supposed to be a fairy tale with the mythical "happily ever after" storybook ending.

The story is all too familiar. You meet someone against all odds and fall in love.

You get engaged and start planning your lives together. You set a date and plan the wedding, including marbled invitations infused with the aroma of Tahitian Vanilla, a wedding cake so tall it requires a safety permit from the city, gilded tablecloths, centerpieces with timeless wild mixes of fresh cut garden roses, and a seating chart so complicated it requires a member of Mensa to decipher it.

That was just the wedding. Whew! Then comes the honeymoon and moving in together. The honeymoon period carries you through until you either have children or stop apologizing for your natural bodily functions, whichever comes first. You balance work and home life, maybe raise children, buy a home, and save for retirement. Then come the seven most repeatable things in every marriage: Monday, Tuesday, Wednesday, Thursday, Friday, Saturday, and Sunday. That's not just my opinion; that's based on solid scientific research.

You had your arguments over the years.

Nothing that every couple doesn't go through. However, you always made up, worked it out, and moved on. Then at some point, something happened that would change the course of your life: the wrecking ball.

The wrecking ball was the sinking realization that your life would no longer be what you thought it would be. It may have built up over time or it came from a sudden event, like an infidelity. Either way, the world you once knew and thought you would live in for the rest of your life would suddenly change dramatically.

What was once comfortable and predictable had now given way to uncertainty.

For most people, divorce is a life-changing event.

It's not a small course correction or something that requires tweaking. Divorce has a major impact on our lives and has the potential to create long-lasting or lifelong effects. Other life-changing events may be the loss of a child, a terminal or chronic health diagnosis, or a catastrophic injury.

Although there are cases when some couples agree that they both fell out of love and both realized that they were not meant to be together and so they divorced amicably while still considering each other as friends, this is the exception and not the rule.

This type of divorce is more of a negotiated exit than a calamity. This is not to minimize their experiences but to say this is not what typically happens.

For most of us, whether through a divorce or a breakup from a long-term relationship, there are multiple stages of grief, anxiety, trauma, restlessness, uncertainty, and heartbreak. The order in which we experience these can differ for everyone. In most cases, they will also overlap and transition from one to another. The severity in which each person in the relationship experiences these can also differ.

Divorce in and of itself is not necessarily punishing: the process is. That process can be divided into three stages: The lead-up to divorce, the divorce process itself, and post-divorce. For now, we only consider this part of the journey that depends on the wrecking ball's swing distance.

It is natural to feel we lack control, especially during such a chaotic period.

You may have heard of Malala Yousafzai. Or maybe you haven't. She was a young girl living in Pakistan who loved attending school, influenced by her father's passion for teaching girls. Her father was a teacher and ran the school in their village. Then in 2008, at 11, she was forced out of school by the Taliban, who prohibited young girls from attending school.

Believing that every girl deserves an education, Malala continued to speak out regarding every girl's right to an education. By following her passion and standing up for her human rights, she was targeted for assassination. In October 2012, returning from the school she longed to attend, a masked gunman boarded her bus, asking where she was. He opened fire and shot her in the head. Only when she woke up 10 days later in the UK did she realize what had happened to her. After months of around-the-clock care, surgeries, and rehab, she rejoined her family at their new home.

What does Malala's story have to do with you, you ask? Well, nothing. Except for the part that happened next.

Having experienced a catastrophic event in her life, she was at a crossroads. She could change course and live quietly, possibly in hiding for the rest of her life or leverage her second chance at life by continuing to follow her passion and devotion to helping young girls worldwide. Like you, she needed to decide if she would let a cataclysmic event change *who she was*.

She decided that it would not change her.

With 130 million girls worldwide out of school, she decided she would continue to fight for herself and all of them.

In 2014, Malala became the youngest recipient of the Nobel Peace Prize for her relentless dedication to work and speaking for those who have been silenced. In 2020, she graduated from Oxford University with a Philosophy, Politics, and Economics degree.

Your divorce or breakup may have changed your circumstances, but you must decide if it will change *who you are*. I use the present tense here, rather than the past, to emphasize that you can still make this decision no matter how long it's been or at what stage of life you are.

It is common for us to lose ourselves in marriage and gradually lose our identity. We go from me to we. That's not necessarily a bad thing. When two people come together and decide to spend the rest of their lives together in a committed relationship, some adjustments need to be made. Both are unique individuals with personalities, characters, morals, beliefs, upbringings, cultural or religious backgrounds, hopes, dreams, and life experiences. Some negotiations and concessions need to be made. How much can depend on how compatible you are with each other.

However, these should be about living conditions, prioritizing time to spend together, agreeing on how to raise children (if applicable), making financial goals, and supporting each other's dreams and passions.

These should never be about changing who you are or what makes you, you.

The success of the marriage or the relationship should never be conditional on giving up who you are or what you care about.

Though many things require compromise, some things are non-negotiable.

Compromise works both ways and is not a one-way street. One-way compromise can best be described as choosing between drinking a glass of water or poison.

You can compromise and have half a glass of each. The result is the same: death. Positive stuff, right?

There is a catch in accepting who you are and expecting that others will too. It means accepting our strengths as well as our weaknesses. If we are open to the idea that someone else must accept our shortcomings, then why are we flexible about them accepting our strengths and individuality?

Why do our hopes and dreams, passions, or personal traits have to be on the chopping block for a relationship to succeed? Doesn't iron sharpen iron? Should partners not draw out and amplify each other's passions and strengths while refining each other's limitations?

Refusing to let your circumstances change who you are does not mean you cannot transform into a better version of yourself. It means you are unwilling to change the core of your identity to suit someone else's agenda.

If each person in the relationship is not willing to accept the core self of the other, then they should consider parting ways for the benefit of both. We are constantly inundated with conflicting messages. We hear the stereotypes about men and women. We watch movies with unrealistic plots and storylines about love.

We hear gossip about divorced friends or family members and how they didn't "meet their former spouse's needs "or "didn't try hard enough" to make the marriage work. And it's all bullshit.

Marriage isn't a contract with an irrevocability clause. If anything, it should confirm mutually assured destruction.

A marriage where anything goes leads to divorce with everything gone. Remaining in a loveless marriage or one that benefits only one partner is a divorce on an installment plan. It's only a matter of time before the wrecking ball of reality destroys the house.

A wrecking ball is used to destroy a building that was abandoned long ago and has outlived its purpose.

For those who are nostalgic, it signifies the unfortunate end of an era by holding on to past glories to determine the present. But to those who are invested in the property and wish to see it reach its full potential, the old building presents a stumbling block to progress and seek its removal.

If we are holding on to what used to be or what might have been, we will never fully be able to move on. As humans, we need things to make sense to process them. We long for closure to fill the void inside us so we can finally understand it and move on. That's why we assign random causes to events we don't understand. He died of cancer because he used to smoke. Her son is on drugs because the parents are never home.

An arbitrary one-liner that is supposed to explain it all away. What we seek is closure. Getting full closure sounds nice, like in the movies where one of the characters gets to talk things out with a loved one in the last moments on that person's deathbed.

They finally make amends, and both people feel a sense of wholeness just before the monitor makes the sound of a long solid beep.

The person remaining cries as they kiss the other on the forehead to say their final goodbye. They feel a sense of closure and are ready to move on.

Real life has other plans. We rarely get what we need at just the right time. If we wait for some subjective cosmic event to occur before we can move on, we will be waiting a long time and stuck in divorce limbo even longer.

How do we move on without feeling the full closure of our divorce tied up in a neat bow? I'm not going to lie, the answer sucks. You move on, not by avoiding the darkness but by walking through it.

It will not be a one-time event or decision but the collection of hundreds of decisions and reactions, each building upon the other, until it becomes autonomous and the past no longer has control over you.

How long should this take? It should take as long as you need. Don't accept some arbitrarily defined time period or deadline by which you must "get over it." This process can't be rushed.

While walking through the darkness, it's natural that you will artificially turn the light on due to fear. That doesn't mean you have failed; you have paused your growth to catch your breath. The important thing is that you regain your courage, turn the light back off, and continue walking through the darkness.

Once your fears dissipate, you will be better prepared to deal with what has been hiding in plain sight all along. You will know when your journey through the darkness is nearing its end: When the light naturally turns on, and you don't even notice.

Divorce is the product of a flawed system, not necessarily flawed people. When a building is in shambles, is it the wrecking ball we blame, or do we question the integrity of the structure?

We need to stop looking at divorce as the problem and start recognizing it as a symptom of the problem. The problem is a broken system of expectations and protocols regarding relationships, love, and marriage.

This does not absolve us of our responsibilities and contributions to the failed relationship. It simply reframes it so we can understand why it happened, instead of simply how it happened.

It's an important distinction. When we focus on how something happened, we can get stuck in the details, losing sight of the bigger picture. We drown ourselves in the minutiae, in all the "he said, she said" of the situation.

It becomes a daunting and never-ending task, and in the end, it's a futile one. Focusing on why it happened allows us to understand our actions, motives, and emotions. It helps us gain insight and clarity on what was driving our behavior and making sense of the other person's behavior.

The 'why' helps us look within and see the parts of ourselves we would rather not confront. The destructive patterns, the insecurities, the fears. We all have our demons; it's just a question of whether we're ready to face them.

When you're going through a divorce, it's easy to feel like the entire universe is against you, that every step forward is followed by two steps back.

But sometimes, it's in these moments of hardship and despair, that we're forced to confront our deepest fears and insecurities, that we're pushed to the edge, where we finally discover who we are and what we're made of.

So, if divorce is the wrecking ball, what's the old, dilapidated building it's set to demolish? It's our old self, our old life, our old mindset, the old "us". The wrecking ball of divorce isn't an instrument of destruction; it's an instrument of change. It demolishes the old so that the new can emerge.

The wrecking ball of divorce is not an enemy; it's an ally. It's the force that propels us from our comfort zone, compels us to change and grow, and creates the space for something new, something better to emerge. When faced with the harsh reality of divorce, it can feel like everything is falling apart, but in reality, it's everything falling into place.

The path ahead may seem dark and treacherous, filled with obstacles and challenges. But every step you take, no matter how small, moves you forward.

As you navigate this path, remember that the darkness isn't a sign of hopelessness; it's a canvas waiting for you to paint your new life upon it.

The darkness of divorce doesn't signify the absence of light; it's a stage for the stars of your strength, resilience, and courage to shine brighter. Don't be afraid of the darkness; embrace it, for it holds the promise of a new dawn, a new beginning.

So, yes, the wrecking ball of divorce may have shattered your world, but it also gave you the chance to rebuild it. To construct a new world, tailored to your dreams, desires, and aspirations. A world that reflects who you truly are, not who you were expected to be. A world where you're the architect of your own destiny.

Divorce isn't the end; it's the beginning of a new chapter in your life, a chapter filled with possibilities, growth, and transformation. It's an opportunity to start anew, to rewrite your story, to redefine who you are and what you want from life.

The wrecking ball of divorce isn't a symbol of destruction; it's a symbol of rebirth, of renewal, of hope.

Your journey through the darkness may be difficult, and at times it may feel unbearable. But remember, the deeper the darkness, the brighter the stars. The more intense your pain, the greater your potential for growth and transformation.

Like the phoenix rising from the ashes, you too will rise from the wreckage of your old life, stronger, wiser, and more resilient. And when you do, you'll realize that the wrecking ball of divorce was not a weapon aimed at your destruction, but a tool designed for your liberation. It's not an end, but a beginning. A chance to build a life that's authentic, fulfilling, and true to who you are.

The process might be painful, the journey might be long, but the reward is invaluable - the opportunity to live your life on your terms, to discover your true potential, and to become the person you were always meant to be.

So, embrace the wrecking ball of divorce, for it holds the key to your transformation.

Chapter 2
Through the Darkness

"It is in isolation that we are least alone."

– Unknown

Isolation gets a bad rap. I'm not talking about physical or social isolation, which can sometimes be damaging and traumatizing. The COVID-19 pandemic and related public health measures, such as social distancing and self-isolation, led to mass loneliness and disconnect. These measures were implemented to slow the spread of a highly contagious virus, but their side effects were real.

The type of isolation that is helpful on our journey is where we are away from distraction and alone with ourselves and our thoughts. It doesn't mean spending less time with loved ones or shutting anyone out of our lives.

It means turning off the white noise in the background, maybe for the first time in our lives.

White noise is an artificial distraction meant to drown out other noises so that they don't disturb us. The problem is that the other noises never stop, and they are trying to tell us something: Let them.

The white noise machines we run in our lives to avoid reality are like closing our eyes to hide from our problems: They don't help us hide; they make us more vulnerable.

In the popular sitcom The Big Bang Theory, one of the main characters, Penny, was notorious for having a check engine light in her car that she constantly ignored. Finally, in one episode, after the check engine light had been on for a long time, her car stopped running while she was driving it. One of the jokes from that scene was that, although her car had died, on the plus side, her check engine light had finally turned off.

A car's check engine light resembles a symbolic check engine light in our lives. How long has your check engine light been on? Maybe it's time to find out why your internal warning system's light is on and take steps to begin to address it.

I'm not going to lie. In reality, paying attention to what's ailing us is extremely uncomfortable. It's not something that comes naturally. We tend to take the path of least resistance.

We distract ourselves in various ways, such as watching television, listening to podcasts, scrolling through endless feeds on social media, watching TikTok videos of cats playing musical instruments, listening to audiobooks, or playing video games. Always busy and in a rush, but actually going nowhere and accomplishing very little.

There's nothing wrong with any of those things, but they should be tools in your arsenal on your journey to self-healing, not replacements instead of.

At best, they can keep you in denial and stunt your growth. At worst, they act as impostors by giving you a false sense of "doing something" while keeping your attention away from what matters.

Like a magician distracting you while he tricks you.

Those distractions are just the tame ones. There is also alcohol abuse, illicit or prescription drug use, gambling, sexual addiction, pornography, food addiction, and toxic anger, to name a few. All of these are used to numb the pain that we feel. In the long run, we grow a tolerance to them and require more to continue numbing the pain. Eventually, they cause new pains, no longer providing the numbing feeling we once sought.

So, we seek new numbing agents. Anything that can turn down the volume of the voices in our heads. Anything that can take us to a different place than we are in now.

We transition from one destructive habit to another.

Alcohol slows our brains running at high speeds, then makes us feel artificial highs, giving us a glimpse of what life used to be like when we were once happy.

Gambling takes our minds off our failures and gives us the highs of adrenaline, always seeking validation that our problems are not of our own doing but *by chance*. And so, we continue to tempt fate, waiting for our lives to improve by the same chance.

Pornography or sexual addiction increases the amount of dopamine our brain releases to compensate for the levels of self-loathing we experience. For being self-conscious. For feeling undesirable. To fantasize about being wanted and to feel like the center of attention.

Toxic anger releases catecholamines to give us short-term energy, giving us a false sense of control. To validate our feelings of self-righteousness. To deal with situations that threaten the perception we have of ourselves.

They are all coping mechanisms that keep us from facing the truth about ourselves. And they are all lies. Deceiving us into believing that we have finally found a way to cope with the darkness in our lives. But lies don't end marriages; the truth does.

If you are struggling with addiction of any kind, you need to seek the proper help you need beyond this book's scope. Addiction recovery is its journey and will require help from those specializing in it.

We are the only ones who can deal with our truth.

Others can offer guidance or support, but the burden of truth is ours to carry. And that frightens us. It makes us feel isolated, but it is in isolation that we are least alone.

Everyone who has ever touched or hurt us comes in and out of our thoughts like a cast of characters, each entering and exiting the stage. We keep replaying scenes from our past over and over again.

We have imaginary conversations with the people in them, trying to replay the scenes more acceptably. We argue with the same people (and win every time.) And yet, nothing changes.

The only way through the darkness is with eyes wide open and the courage to change. Why do we need to change? Because if nothing needs to change, why do we feel so miserable and empty?

We might feel as though we are fine and that there is nothing wrong with how we are dealing with our hurts. But at some point, we need to realize that if we keep doing what we are doing, we will keep getting what we've been getting.

Don't confuse the need to change with accepting responsibility for every wrong done to you. It doesn't mean giving up control. It means that you dare to take it back. The decision to change and take back control of your life can be hard and it's hard for a reason: Something is at stake.

Your marriage and eventual divorce have left you with scars, whether you can see them or not. These scars can be from your spouse, or they can be self-inflicted.

When we look at those scars, they are constant reminders of the pain we felt when we were first wounded. We have a hard time accepting those scars. We want to either tear them off or cover them up.

Our refusal to accept the scars is the inability to accept ourselves as who we are now, not who we used to be. We keep wanting to go back in time and undo the hurt. We want those who hurt us to return what they did or said. We feel a sense of injustice that needs to be corrected.

Our sense of justice is built into our DNA. We know what's right, and we know what's wrong, and when justice isn't served, we get angry.

We tend to stay angry as long as the injustice persists. Anger gives you a sense of control. That it's the anger that gives you the strength to move on, and we stay in anger because to do otherwise would feel like we would be betraying ourselves.

The anger allows us to go back in time and relive the hurt repeatedly, like on a video set to playback. By doing so, we are constantly reopening the wound, expecting the person that hurt us to close the wound, like a surgery that leaves no scars.

"Do not look for healing at the feet of those who broke you" - Rupi Kaur.

Our anger is never satisfied because it never can be. We tell ourselves that we can only ever achieve justice through vengeance. If we go down, we are taking them down with us.

You may fantasize about exacting revenge upon them.

"Before embarking on a journey of revenge, dig two graves." – Confucius

Plotting revenge poisons our mind and creates an unhealthy obsession that leads to our own destruction. The best revenge is living well and to be successful in what we do. That sounds like a terrible movie plot, but reality works differently.

"I'll take them to the brink of financial ruin," you say. "I'll take away their home and their car. I'll get them fired from their job. I'll destroy the relationship they are currently in. I'll badmouth them and ruin their reputation."

That sounds like a Charles Bronson movie (and sounds pretty good) but then what? We are still left with the scars. The very scars that made us angry, to begin with.

Our anger is a refusal to heal. Because to heal would feel like we are letting them off the hook. Like we are exonerating them from their betrayal and their actions. It would mean that we are no longer victims. Except that isn't true.

If we are honest with ourselves, we will see that we are angry because we are scared. The anger just masks the fear.

We're scared about moving on and about what the future holds. We are scared about who we will be once the hurt heals. We have identified with our hurts for so long that our identity will be threatened.

Let it go.

Letting go isn't easy. It doesn't happen on the day you decide to let go. It means letting go every day.

There is an ancient story about capturing monkeys in the wild. The hunter places a cage with narrow bars in the forest. In the cage is a banana. The monkey comes along, reaches into the cage with his hand, and grabs the banana. However, the banana is too large to fit through the cage bars. The monkey could free himself by letting go of the banana and freeing his arm. But the monkey will not let go and is trapped by the hunter.

Let go of the banana.

Holding on is a self-imposed sentence, denying us the freedom to seek what is good for us.

There is a path to letting go of the anger, but it is not easy: Forgiveness.

However, this isn't the kind of forgiveness you get from a priest. This forgiveness is accepting that your healing and restoration are more important than wishing restiveness on the person who hurt you. Because you can't have both. As long as you are angry, forgiveness is improbable.

Forgiveness means letting go of the anger that has numbed your pain so far. It shifts the responsibility for healing and our future happiness from the person who caused the hurt to you. It means no longer waiting for the person who hurt you to be the person who heals you. That is a burden you must carry.

The healing process doesn't depend on those who caused the hurt. It depends on the person hurt emotionally, psychologically, spiritually, or mentally. This is the part of the journey that is yours to embark on and to take alone.

The journey from anger to peace is a long one. You draw from forgiveness along your journey to give you the strength to carry on one more day.

The temptation to flip back and forth between forgiveness and anger will be strong. It's hard to give up what we once thought brought us comfort. That's because forgiveness is a process, not a one-time event. Forgiveness opens the prison gates so that the hurt can escape.

Forgiveness, in and of itself, does not grant you parole from the prison in your mind. It gives you a path toward freedom from your hurts, so they no longer victimize you. It means accepting that the past can never be changed. We can never go back and do things differently, take back a hurtful word, or play out a different scenario of what might have been.

It means accepting that the scars you bear are from those who have impacted your life and that the onus is on you to wear them.

It means accepting who you are now, not because of, but despite those scars. It's a decision to take back control and create your destiny.

You do not need anyone else's approval to do this.

You are on this leg of the journey alone and can decide which paths you take along the way. You do not need to have a conversation and formally tell the person you are setting yourself free from that you are forgiving them.

Remember that this is not about them; it's about you.

The pain you are feeling is not imagined; it's real and may be making you emotionally sick. Don't let others wave your pain away; more importantly, don't deny your own pain. It's through the pain, through the hurt, and through the unfairness of it all that we make it to the other side and finally heal. There is no easy way through this. There is no shortcut along the journey. People don't heal from wellness; people heal from sickness.

It is through the darkness that we encounter our greatest fears. But we see a dark shadow in the distance when we dare to change, stay the course, and continue despite our fears.

As our eyes adjust through the darkness and we inch closer, we see that the dark shadow in the distance isn't a frightening figure, it is a reflection of ourselves upon which our fears were cast.

Let it go.

Accept who you are today, and choose to make peace with the you of yesterday.

When we face our own reflection, we come to understand that we are not the product of the actions of others, but the sum of our own decisions. We control our narrative. We have the power to decide that we will not be defined by the pain we've experienced but by the strength it took to endure it.

Each of us has our scars, both visible and hidden. They are not simply reminders of the wounds we've suffered. Instead, they are badges of survival, of resilience.

They tell the story of how we have overcome and grown, how we've navigated the treacherous waters of our lives, how we have loved, how we have lost, how we have grieved, how we have raged, and how, most importantly, we have continued.

We must accept that our past is unchangeable. No amount of anger, resentment, or vengefulness can alter what has happened.

Instead of sinking into the despair of wishing things were different, use your energy to forge a new path forward. Instead of sinking into the tar pit of resentment, learn to swim in the ocean of forgiveness.

In the depths of our pain, we often fail to realize that forgiveness is a gift we give ourselves. When we free ourselves from the shackles of anger, we find a new path open to us—a path that leads to acceptance and ultimately healing.

We must understand that this is not a sprint but a marathon. It's not about quickly getting to the finish line but staying on course even when the road gets tough, when the wind howls, and the rain pours.

It's about endurance and persistence, even when every step feels like it's through quicksand. It's about recognizing that the journey itself can be its reward and that every step is a victory in its own right.

On this journey, we may stumble and fall. We might lose our way, but that doesn't mean we've lost the battle. It only means that the journey is hard, and it's okay to struggle.

It's okay to feel weary and broken because that's what makes us human. You see, it's easy to remain angry and bitter. It's much harder to forgive, to move on, and to heal. That's why the path of forgiveness is the road less traveled. But those who dare to take this path often discover a resilience and strength within themselves they never knew existed.

The shadows of our past can either oppress us with their weight or inspire us with their testament to our resilience. The choice is ours to make. We can allow our past to control our present and dictate our future, or we can seize control and chart our course.

Letting go of the anger and resentment is not about forgetting what happened but about remembering without letting it rule you. It's about accepting the past, acknowledging the pain, and deciding to move forward despite it all.

You don't need anyone's validation to embark on this journey. All you need is the courage to step forward and the conviction that you deserve peace, joy, and healing.

You don't have to wait for others to mend what they've broken within you. The power to heal is within you. You just have to muster the courage to use it.

So, in the hushed whispers of solitude, listen to the call of your own heart. In the throbbing silence of your pain, find your own rhythm. In the hidden crevices of your wounds, discover your own strength.

Embrace the darkness and face your fears. Because it's only in the darkness that we can truly appreciate the beauty of the stars. It's only in the silence that we can hear the sound of our own heartbeat. It's only when we are alone with our thoughts that we can truly find ourselves.

Remember, in isolation, we are least alone. So let go of your anger, embrace forgiveness, and journey on. The path may be long and treacherous, but it's worth the journey. Because, in the end, it leads to a place of healing, of peace, and of a self-acceptance that's more liberating than any vengeance could ever be. Let it go.

Chapter 3
Letting Go

"*Only by acceptance of the past will you alter its meaning.*"

– *T.S. Elliot*

There is comfort in holding on. It allows us to believe that the past can be altered.

If we hold on, we can change the course of history or write a new ending to the story.

It allows us to examine its meaning. It grants us the ability to question our perception of it. We give ourselves a lot of leeway to see it from different angles. It permits us to be flexible in our interpretation of it.

It still allows us the freedom to doubt where we were once sure.

We get to re-interview those who were there like a collection of witness statements. We get to take what we like and leave the rest. The comfort comes from believing we can rewrite the past and alter the present.

But the present isn't changing, is it? You may have a different job since your divorce or live in a new city, but the past seems to follow you wherever you go. You pack it gently, like with your dishes or a fragile object. Always making sure it makes the journey with you without a scratch or dent.

And yet the past haunts you. It is in your dreams if you are determined enough to avoid your past. It pops up when you see someone in public who reminds you of someone from your past.

Or when you hear a name similar to theirs. Or when a certain song is playing while shopping at a department store.

Some of the memories are fairly harmless.

Like when you shared a good meal or got a flat tire on the highway and ended up laughing about it. Other memories from our past can shake us to our core and stop us dead in our tracks.

When I was around ten years old, I was a bit of a free spirit. Walking around the house (or the yard) in my underwear was not a big deal.

I was the class clown, always looking for the next joke to tell or the next impression I could make of a famous person, so I could get a laugh from my friends, family, or classmates. I looked up to those who were older and acted the same way. They were my mentors, showing me that my positivity and sense of humor could make me as likable as they were. Everybody wants to be around Winnie the Pooh, not Eeyore, I thought.

That summer, one of my favorite family members was coming to visit us from out of town. My family would typically be the ones to travel to visit, but this time, he was coming to visit us. The guy who would wear wigs with me at department stores to get strange looks from the other shoppers or who would dress up and pretend to be Michael Jackson while out in public (the resemblance was uncanny) was now coming to spend 2 weeks with us. Score!

It was going to be the greatest summer of our lives. Who would we prank, and what kind of crap would we get into? I was ten, and he was sixteen. He brought a certain level of legitimacy to our shenanigans.

During his visit, our old neighbors who lived next door to us for years dropped by for a visit, along with their kids, who were about the same age as me and my sister. It was good to see them, as it had been a while. We reconnected instantly and spent most of the time catching up and discussing what was new with them and us.

After they left, it was back to my older family member who came for a visit. Our family had a pool in the backyard, and we spent much time swimming. We'd play all kinds of different games in the pool.

If people were home, they'd be in the pool, and we had a blast.

Later that day, everybody returned inside, leaving me and my older relative alone in the pool. That was when the darkness began.

He asked me about our former neighbors who had just visited. He told me he saw me and one of the girls having sex. I responded by telling him I didn't know what he was talking about (and being 10 years old, I didn't even know how to do what he said I did.)

He was adamant about what he said he saw and that he would tell my parents. I was mortified. Not only did I not know what he was talking about, he was about to tell my parents about something so terrible about me. As he exited the pool to go "tell" my parents, I yelled for him to stop.

He came back into the pool while approaching me with the grin of the Cheshire Cat. He had me right where he wanted me. He groomed me into the corner he was always planning for me in his sick mind.

At that moment, even though I had no idea what he had planned for me, my heart sank as the dark clouds began rolling in.

He told me then that he would go to my parents unless I did what he said. So, he led me up to my bedroom and closed the door.

We were inside for about an hour, but it may as well have been 2 years. He did things to me that I can never undo and made me see things that I can never unsee.

I fought back many times, but his age and strength overpowered me.

When he finished, he put his clothes back on and left the room. I lay on my bed in a catatonic state for an amount of time that I will never know.

What shook me from that catatonic state was my mom yelling for me up the stairs. It was dinner time. As I reached the bottom of the stairwell, I saw everyone sitting at the dining room table. And it looked no different than any other day. I turned around and went to the bathroom instead. When I entered the bathroom, I immediately locked the door. I felt sick and thought I was going to vomit. Attempting to avoid throwing up, I splashed cold water on my face over and over again.

My bangs were now wet with all the water splashed.

As I watched beads of water streaming down my face in the mirror, the feeling of getting sick had passed, but the feelings of dizziness set in. I lay down on the bathroom floor, staring up at the ceiling until I fully regained consciousness.

Then I got up, took a deep breath, walked out of the bathroom, and headed for the dining room table.

I sat down at the table and stared at my plate. As time passed, I realized that the dinner conversation was as it always was: Telling a few jokes and talking about the day's events.

My predator took part in all of it without hesitation or remorse.

I realized then that although the world around me was the same, I was different now. The voices around the table began to muffle, drowned out by new voices in my head. I was no longer the free spirit and positive person I once was.

The abuse continued daily, sometimes multiple times a day. It got to the point where I got used to being raped. My consciousness would convert to a catatonic state at the first signal of what would take place like a doctor inducing a patient into a coma to relieve pain and trauma in the patient with acute injuries.

Finally, the day came when his visit had ended, and he was leaving. I watched incredulously as everyone was saying goodbye.

He barely acknowledged me as he left, which was fine, as I had nothing to say in return. Watching him drive away that day, I felt the slight breeze of freedom, oblivious to the fact that I was only beginning my sentence for a crime I did not commit.

At its core, the past is a series of good or bad events frozen in time. We can attach meaning to it or insignificance, but we cannot undo, add, subtract, or alter the events contained within it. We can change the story we tell ourselves or others, but we cannot hide from the truth of it. We know what happened. And until we face it, it will continue to affect us whether we want it to.

Like the passengers of Flight 180 in the movie Final Destination, who avoided death in a plane crash, only to eventually fall victim, one by one, unable to escape their fate.

How do we deal with the truth of our past or divorce? We face it by accepting it. That doesn't mean we agree with it or take responsibility for it. It means that we face the difficult feelings that come with it. The ones we have been avoiding because they are uncomfortable.

"Holding on is believing that there's only a past. Letting go is knowing that there's a future." – Daphne Rose Kingma.

Stop traveling back in time or alternating universes. Live in the present, which is hard, unfamiliar, and unfair. Allow yourself to fully feel the hurt. Completely feel the unfairness of it all. Fully experience the humiliation.

You will have a tendency to want to go back to what is comfortable. Resist it. Don't turn back, and don't avoid it. Embrace the shame and the loneliness. Don't give up on the last mile in the first leg of your journey.

Don't wait until you are stronger or until there is a better time. There is no better time. Like it or not, time is the subtle thief of youth. And healing from your divorce or what is making you emotionally sick is not inevitable. Don't tell yourself that it's going to be easy.

Don't run out of the clock by trying to keep yourself busy getting hung up on every subject or academic reference to the truth of your past.

On the road to recovery and wholeness, it will feel like you are walking through the valley of the shadow of death. Because you are. Face the fear.

Although you will walk this part of the journey alone, and it may not be your first choice to do so, it is the lesser of all evils. If it was easy, you would have done it by now.

There will be days when it feels like you are in mourning because you are. But you are not mourning the loss of the person who hurt you. You are mourning the loss of the person who once loved you.

You must accept that it's over and separate yourself from the people you have lost, or you will be doomed to stay confined with them.

Accepting what happened to you doesn't remove your scars.

It means that you accept that you *are* scarred. Make the decision not to be miserable for the rest of your life because someone wronged you.

Accept the burden that they placed upon you. Carrying that burden will make you stronger.

What does this look like in practice? Accept the fact that they are never coming back.

The marriage you once had, or thought you had, is over. Accept the fact that someone out there knows intimate details about you. Don't wait for them to carry the load. Make decisions for yourself without their input, either real or imagined.

Focus on the time you have left rather than the time that has elapsed. Don't let your past rob you of your present and future. Don't replace the person you lost with someone else (not at first.)

There is a void, and you are the one who needs to fill it. You need to feel whole first.

Rekindle relationships that were lost or start new friendships. You accept that one day, letting go will feel natural and barely noticeable.

You start by replacing the squares on your crochet blanket one at a time. It will feel strangely liberating. Eventually, you will have a new design, connections, memories, and life.

Let go.

Chapter 4
Moving On

"We cannot change the past, but we can start a new chapter with a happy ending."

– Nishan Panwar

Acceptance of the past allows us to alter its meaning, but that does not immediately erase the emotions attached. This takes time.

One of the most common emotions we experience during this time is sadness. The sadness we feel is a normal part of this process. It means that we are accepting our reality. It is a healthy part of the change. We cannot let ourselves just "get over it." We can't lie to ourselves or let ourselves believe that we can maintain a sense of joy and happiness through it, all while drowning out our grief.

We feel a sense of loss. We are no longer trying to bargain our way out of it. This is where it feels darkest before dawn. This is where we need to allow ourselves to grieve. To permit ourselves to feel.

Where we allow ourselves to feel uncomfortable, despite the urge to escape. Because there is no escape hatch. No ejection buttons. This is where it becomes real, and the fear sets in. The fear of the unknown. The fear of being alone. The fear of no one having our backs. The fear of who we will be on the other side.

Where we dispense or discard every cliché about moving on and about how every day is a new day. That it is better to have loved and lost than to never have loved at all.

About how life goes on. About how time heals all wounds. This is where we feel the emptiness of it all. Where we realize that the collection of common knowledge and throw-away one-liners are empty shells and where we feel the cold hollowness of the wisdom we so cherished and once dispensed to others with abandon.

Where we realize that the concept of time is meaningless, that arbitrary time periods for grieving are bullshit attempts to short-circuit the pain we experience.

The sadness we feel in our hearts is part of our healing journey. That our heart is rebuilding its capacity to love again. Where we realize that we are not unlovable, that we are not unattractive, that we are not unwanted, where we realize that we are not broken, our heart is.

We realize that the tears in our eyes and the droplets down our faces are not a sign of weakness but a physical manifestation of our pain escaping to the outside, where we are more vulnerable. Where we no longer care about social norms.

Where we seek comfort in what we once shunned.

Where we walk through the doors we once avoided. Where we face the darkness we once feared. Where we open the windows we once covered.

Where we need to be alone. Where isolation feels more humane than any other alternative. Where loneliness feels imprisoning and freeing at once. Where we are no longer waiting for someone else to guide us.

Where we have the natural capacity to connect with others who are grieving. Where we no longer sympathize but empathize.

Through it all, we allow ourselves the facility to move on.

"You cannot protect yourself from sadness without protecting yourself from happiness." – Jonathan Safran Foer.

When I was 18, I fell deeply in love with a girl down the street. Whenever I came into her presence, I would forget my name or how to speak. She would ask me a question, and I would be speechless. I thought about her constantly and finally mustered the courage to ask her out. To my amazement, she said yes. The next few months were sheer bliss. Where I was once searching for words, I became a chatterbox.

I always worked so hard to impress her.

She had a bit of a wild side and a rebellious spirit, so I tried playing the bad boy role. I got a haircut that would make my grandmother shriek. I bought a motorcycle and would pick her up at her parent's house. We would cruise downtown or down the highway along the riverfront. Sometimes at high speed, so she would feel a thrill.

I was always in awe of her beauty. Even months later, I was still shy around her.

I knew she was out of my league, so I didn't want to make sudden movements and scare her off. In the end, the worse happened. She broke it off with me. I didn't realize it then, but my timidness turned her off. I tried to be the Barney from How I Met Your Mother, who played it cool but ended up being the Ted, the proverbial nice guy looking for love in all the wrong places.

So, I was relegated to the friend zone. And it hit me hard. It wasn't unusual for me to get friend zoned. I'd lived in that zone for most of my youth, but it felt different this time. I stayed in a state of delusion for a while. She went out with me once, I thought. She'll go out with me again someday. I renounced any attempt by other girls to make their way into my heart.

She was the one, I told myself.

Until she wasn't.

The day she started going out with my best friend was the day I lost it. That's when reality actually hit me. From the day she broke up with me until the day reality hit, I kept trying to keep my spirits up with delusional thoughts and wishful thinking.

But my spirits weren't up during that time. I was miserable and avoiding it. And now, the chickens had come home to roost.

I spent the next while holed up in my bedroom.

Some of my friends or coworkers would try to make me feel better, but none of it worked. I was numb. I would be in my room and sit in silence. I was invited to all kinds of outings but refused them all. I would lay in my bed and blankly stare at the ceiling. At first, I would replay some of my memories of her during happier times on a loop in my head. Then I tried to figure out what I could have done differently. Nothing worked.

I didn't realize it then, but I was experiencing extreme sadness at the loss. Food or drink didn't matter anymore. There is no doubt that I was experiencing a kind of depression. As I lay in my bed, I came to accept that getting her back would never happen. It was very disheartening. The tears would stream down my face. I didn't want anyone to try to make me feel better because they couldn't. Being that young, I didn't know what I was going through.

I was experiencing the sadness that comes from loss. Profound loss. And I was not in a hurry. There was something about processing this loss that felt strangely healing.

After an indeterminate amount of time of laying in bed weeping, thinking it was all over, I suddenly got up. I still remember that day. I threw the covers off of me and opened my bedroom door.

The sun was shining from the hallway outside my bedroom. It was my first time seeing it in I don't know how long. As I looked out into the sunlight and took deep breaths, I thought it was over. I could actually feel the instantaneous of that moment. I was finally free. The dark cloud had finally lifted. I had finally accepted the loss of my girlfriend. I will never forget that experience.

On the outside, it may seem like a trite experience. A love lost during youth. Doesn't everyone have those? Is that really unique? How does that compare to a ten-year marriage? Yes, no, and it doesn't by some arbitrary measure. But that is the point, isn't it? It is our pain, our past, our sadness. We don't wait for validation to experience feelings of loss and sadness.

Acceptance of the past prepares us for the present.

And the present is the only place we live. We cannot live 5 days or 5 years ago, nor can we live 6 months from now. In this universe, the present is today. And we don't get a different universe. We get the one that is here and now.

"It's sad when someone you know becomes someone you knew." – Henry Rollins.

Some people are in our lives for a reason, and some for a season. Who are we to say with certainty which is which? Love was supposed to be forever until it wasn't. All we know is that we are here now. And we are forging our own path. Holding our own hand. By letting things change and not looking back.

You move on by letting yourself be you again.

By morphing back from we to me.

Don't try to stay the married person you once were. You need to make room in your heart to love yourself again and, eventually, someone else.

You move on by finding your independence and being OK with it. By making decisions for yourself. By finding your own voice and using it. By taking pride in your new autonomy. By taking the time to heal and grow.

Take solace that you are now free to pursue passions you never could. To travel to lands you never did. That a whole new world of possibilities has opened up for you. This was not your first choice, but it is the one you have now.

Let the sadness wash over you like a waterfall and fully envelope you. Let your tears cleanse you from your loss. Let the fears you once had seem like a distant memory.

We are stronger now because we were once weaker. And we have become better people because we were once loved.

Let that be enough for now.

"When you're happy, you enjoy the music. When you're sad, you understand the lyrics." – Frank Ocean.

Chapter 5

Through the Looking Glass

"Divorce is just part of your life. It doesn't define who you are. You decide that."

– Karen Finn

Divorce is not a punishment, but the process can feel like it. Or it can be, depending on your point of view. Some have described that process as equivalent to a proctological procedure or all the fun of a root canal. And it's not as uncommon as you might think. When going through a divorce, it can feel like we are one of the few experiencing this process or that most other people don't know what it's like.

Researchers estimate that 40% to 50% of all first marriages end in divorce or permanent separation. That number increases to about 60% to 65% for second marriages. We are not alone. That's not supposed to make you feel better. It just shows that we are not the outlier.

Not only are we dealing with a slew of emotions, but we are also treading new ground. And as we look around at others who have gone through a divorce, it's not encouraging. No one goes through a divorce bragging about it being the greatest and most enriching experience they have ever had (with few exceptions). Your separation period is when you physically parted ways. The divorce is the final agreement on that partition process. It can feel like one of the darkest periods of your life.

In reality, marriage was a contract for life that you got into with the other person. Divorce is simply breaking the contract and dispensing its obligations. I'm not trying to be cold and clinical about it, but that's the reality of divorce. And it is amazing how little control you have over the outcome.

Most jurisdictions have laws and regulations to deal with a divorce's financial and legal obligations. A lot of formulas and actuarial tables are interesting for those who work in that field, but they can cause extreme boredom in the rest of us. It is stunning how little control over this process either party has to begin with.

This isn't to say that you shouldn't stick up for your own rights. But once both parties' rights have been exercised, the leftover gap is usually not much. It's like politicians running in elections within a two-party system. They each have about 40% of the vote right out of the gate without having to do very much. What they're fighting over is the leftover 20% of the vote. That 20% gap is what most couples end up fighting over in a divorce that can last years.

Divorce can sometimes be messy and time-consuming, but it has no bearing on who you are, your worth as a human being, or your present and future happiness. Attaching some greater significance to the divorce process is a waste of your time and an insult to your soul.

Most of the divorce process is about dispensing assets and any future compensatory obligations, such as alimony. These are the necessary evils in the dissolution of a marriage contract. Don't get too hung up on winning or losing the divorce. There is no winning in divorce. There may be somebody who files for divorce first, or somebody who walks away with more assets, or somebody who might get custody of a shared possession, but no one walks away actually winning.

We see similar scenarios play out in the dispensation of a will or an estate. It may be a group of people clawing to get a bigger share of the estate than the other. Or fighting for years to get possession of a piece of furniture. People end up fighting over items with some arbitrary random significance to them that I guarantee no one will care about in a hundred years because we will all be dead by then.

You need to ask yourself what is actually most important to you. Don't follow the lead of other people or think about what society says you should care about. Ask yourself what you need and what you actually care about. That is what you should focus on during this process.

"It's not the load that breaks down; it's the way you carry it."
– Lena Horne.

One consideration that is rarely thought of is the consumption of time. Time is actually one of the most valuable resources. You can always make more money but can't add more time to your life. The sands of time aren't exactly flowing up the hourglass.

So why spend years in some divorce purgatory, wasting the precious time you have left here on earth? There is a saying that youth is wasted on the young. Youth is also wasted in divorce. Let's face it: There is no sense in beating a dead horse (not that there is any sense in beating a live horse either, but I digress.)

In your old age, will you look back and wish you had gotten more money out of a divorce or could get back some of those years you lost in your youth?

Acceptance of the past means that you can alter its meaning. Someone who accepts that the marriage is over and wants to move on with their life doesn't sweat the small stuff. Nor do they have any interest in prolonging the inevitable.

You can decide how much time, energy, and emotional currency you will expend during the divorce process.

Sometimes, not everything in a divorce is about money. It may not be because we actually want something but because we don't want the other person to have it. How much sense does that make? I'll take mutually assured destruction for $200, Alex.

What about having to pay alimony? What about it? So what? It's a legal requirement, just like paying taxes. Chances are, depending on the jurisdiction, if you are paying alimony, you are the one that either made most of the money or all of the money during the marriage. If that's the case, you have the least to worry about. You know how to make money, save money, and invest money.

You will take those skills with you on your journey to your new life. They served you well in the past, and they will serve you again in the future. If you can create wealth and maintain it, along with a good work ethic, you will make it all back and then some.

There is a reason why most people who win the lottery lose it all within a few short years. It doesn't matter how much they have won. It could be $10,000 or $1,000,000. It's because they didn't know how to manage money before they won. Hence they didn't know how to manage money after they won. People who know how to manage money don't play the lottery, which is why they have money.

Rather than paying alimony, you could be sponsoring a seal or a polar bear in the wild. Or donate it to a charity. Instead, you are supporting another human being in this world. There are worse things for you to spend your money on.

Be glad about that. What does it profit you to gain material possessions but lose your soul or peace of mind?

You have a new life to plan for. Don't let what you can't control rob you of that.

You have a future ahead of you. Take solace in the things that you cannot change.

Don't let divorce drive you to resentment. Resentment is an anger that you feel over and over again. It is angry about something unfair in the past, and you can't let it go. It is mostly because of inaction on our part.

We have regrets about something we failed to address in the past or about missed opportunities. Those regrets can make us feel bad about ourselves, and they can create feelings of guilt. It is because of unresolved guilt that we carry resentments.

And those resentments can creep into our everyday lives and poison our thoughts and words. How do you try to avoid building resentment during your divorce? First, do no harm. Don't go out of your way to make life harder for your former spouse. What is it about the love you once had that you are now ashamed of? So, the marriage didn't work out. Focus on your good times and let that guide your attitude during this process.

Are they the parent of your children? Then for your children's sake, treat their parents with respect by not gossiping or speaking ill of them. And do your kids a favor: Keep them out of this. They don't need to know all the details of the divorce or be made to feel like they need to choose sides. One of the things we tell our kids when announcing the separation is that it doesn't change the fact that they are our children and that they will always have two parents. Let them have two parents.

Second, don't take out your anger for your failings on everyone around you, especially your children. Some people think: "Every time I look at my children, I see my spouse in them." Well, OK.

Isn't that how nature works?

Would you rather they look like some total rando you've never met? Rather than see your former spouse in your children, see yourself in them. If your high school gym teacher was correct, they are just as much you as the other parent.

Remember that the divorce process should not define you.

Let the legal obligations play themselves out. You have no control over them anyway. Don't dwell on whether you agree with your obligations or not. That is a fruitless exercise about if onlys or what ifs. You are about to embark on the next chapter of the rest of your life. Do so with dignity and the ability to keep your head held high. How you think and act during your divorce (and post-divorce) can affect what that next chapter looks like. Chances are, other people will see it too.

See your divorce as the end of your old life and a gateway to the new. Look forward to a new beginning, a new adventure, a new hope, and new opportunities for love again. Envision your future. Focus on the years you have left rather than the years that have already passed.

Prepare for your new destiny.

At times, during the divorce process, you may find yourself looking in the mirror, seeing a stranger staring back at you. The person who was so sure of their future, who committed to another person with undying love, seems a distant figure lost in the fog of change.

But remember, that stranger is still you. It's just a version of you that is scarred, bruised, and perhaps a little fearful. It is a version of you that is being tested. That test isn't necessarily about enduring the pain but about learning, growing, and transforming from the experience.

Your identity may have been tied up with being a spouse, and now that title is being stripped away. But you are more than that. You are an individual with unique talents, dreams, passions, and capabilities.

Divorce doesn't take away the person you were before marriage; it only asks that you rediscover and reclaim that person again.

Often, we romanticize the past, the "what ifs" and "if onlys." This reminiscing tends to gloss over the pain and exaggerate the joy. It's essential to remember that the past had its share of troubles, and the relationship ended for valid reasons.

Do not get entrapped in the nostalgia that distorts the reality of your past. Your memories are pieces of the past; they should be cherished, but not at the cost of your present and future.

Instead, you should channel your energy and time into the process of healing. Learn to forgive - your spouse, and more importantly, yourself. Forgiveness isn't about absolution; it's about freedom - freedom from anger, guilt, and bitterness that binds you to the past. As you forgive, you free yourself to move forward without carrying the weight of the past.

Furthermore, redefine your goals and dreams, which may have been neglected during your married life. This is the perfect time to take up a new hobby, pursue an exciting career path, or simply engage in activities that make you happy. This period of self-exploration can be the most empowering aspect of divorce, as it allows you to truly own your life and define your destiny.

Seek help and support. Reach out to friends, family, and even professionals. We are social creatures, and during tough times, having a supportive network can help us heal and move forward.

Understand that your emotional wellbeing is paramount. It's okay to feel hurt, it's okay to grieve, and it's okay to feel lost. These are all valid responses to a significant life event. But with time, the pain will lessen, the fog will clear, and a stronger, wiser you will emerge.

In the ashes of your old life, a phoenix is ready to rise and embrace the next phase of its existence. Life post-divorce isn't the end; it's a chance to recreate yourself, your relationships, and your future.

Lastly, remember, every dark cloud has a silver lining, and divorce is no exception. The person you become on the other side of this emotional turmoil may surprise you in the best possible way. Embrace the transformation, for through this change, you are given an opportunity to reinvent your life, leaving behind the parts that no longer serve you and moving towards a future where you are in control.

Yes, divorce is a painful process, one that tests your resilience, but it doesn't need to consume you. It is an ending, but every ending is a new beginning.

A new beginning that is entirely in your hands. This transition isn't easy, but it's within your power to navigate through it with grace and emerge stronger and wiser.

You have the power to shape your life beyond divorce. Focus on your growth, your happiness, and your wellbeing, for these are what truly define you.

After all, through the looking glass of divorce, there is a brighter future waiting. Just believe in your strength, value your worth, and keep moving forward.

As Karen Finn said, "Divorce is just part of your life. It doesn't define who you are. You decide that."

Chapter 6: Rebuilding Your Support System

"If we want to be loved, we are looking for a support system. If we want to love, we are looking for spiritual growth."

– Ayya Khema

The journey of life is seldom taken alone. It is our relationships, the network of people we surround ourselves with, that can significantly impact our growth, happiness, and resilience. This chapter, titled "Rebuilding Your Support System", focuses on how you can reinforce your connections with existing friends and family, explore new support systems, and cultivate a new network of like-minded individuals.

In this phase of rebuilding, you may face various challenges and adjustments. Therefore, it becomes crucial to have a strong support system in place to guide you, provide emotional comfort, and challenge you to continue growing.

From recognizing the importance of your current relationships to identifying potential new social circles, this chapter aims to provide a comprehensive guide to enhancing your interpersonal relationships. The importance of support groups is also highlighted, along with techniques to find and engage effectively within them. With the right approaches, you can construct a solid social foundation that facilitates personal development and happiness.

Strengthening Connections with Friends and Family

As humans, we are inherently social creatures. We thrive on connection, and it is often our relationships with friends and family that bring us the most joy, provide us with a sense of belonging, and give us the strength to face life's challenges. This section will guide you through the process of strengthening these essential connections.

Recognizing the Importance of Existing Relationships

Every relationship we hold is like a thread in the fabric of our lives. Some threads are more vibrant or durable, while others may be more subtle or delicate.

Each one, however, contributes to the whole. Existing relationships, with friends and family alike, form the foundation of our support system. Recognizing their importance is the first step in strengthening these connections. Your existing relationships are deeply rooted in shared experiences and memories. These relationships have seen you grow and change, offering support during your low points and celebrating with you during your highs. The comfort of familiarity that these relationships offer cannot be understated. It's a reassurance that you are understood, accepted, and loved for who you are.

Yet, it's easy to take these existing relationships for granted. The busyness of life can often lead us to neglect these connections, causing them to weaken over time. Recognizing the importance of these relationships serves as a reminder to continually invest time and effort into maintaining and strengthening these bonds. After all, they serve as your immediate source of support and companionship, an essential component of your overall wellbeing.

Cultivate gratitude for these relationships and make a conscious effort to acknowledge their importance in your life. This recognition alone can make you more attentive and engaged in these interactions, helping you to further strengthen these connections.

Techniques for Re-engaging with Friends and Family

While recognizing the importance of existing relationships is vital, it is equally crucial to engage actively with your friends and family. Here are some strategies that can help you reconnect and reinforce these bonds:

Regular Communication: Life's responsibilities can often lead to lapses in communication. However, making a habit of regular contact - be it through phone calls, texts, emails, or face-to-face meetups - can keep you connected. Small check-ins can mean a lot, demonstrating that you're thinking of them and that you care.

Active Listening: Make an effort to listen more when you engage with your loved ones. Active listening involves giving your full attention, showing empathy, and providing feedback.

This practice strengthens the connection between you and the other person, as it demonstrates respect and genuine interest in their thoughts and feelings.

Share Experiences: Engaging in shared experiences, such as watching a movie together, going for a walk, or even cooking a meal, can create memorable moments that can help tighten the bonds. Such activities can give you things to talk about and can lead to deeper, more meaningful conversations.

Show Appreciation: A little appreciation can go a long way in maintaining healthy relationships. Regularly express your gratitude for their support and companionship. Such gestures show that you value their role in your life and can contribute significantly to strengthening your relationships.

Openness and Honesty: Honesty is the bedrock of any strong relationship. Be open about your feelings, concerns, and thoughts. Sharing your vulnerabilities can deepen your connections and promote a mutual understanding that can weather even the toughest of times.

Remember, the purpose of these techniques is to maintain and enhance the depth and quality of your connections with your loved ones. Relationships are an evolving entity, always growing and changing. These techniques offer a framework to guide that evolution in a positive and strengthening direction.

Handling Possible Changes in These Relationships

There's a universal truth we all have to face sooner or later: change is inevitable. However, when it comes to relationships with friends and family, these changes can be daunting. It's crucial to handle these shifts with grace, understanding, and flexibility.

Embrace the Change: It's easy to fall into a routine, especially with long-standing relationships. But as life evolves, so too do our relationships. Accepting this fact, instead of resisting it, will help you adapt more easily to these changes. Remember, growth is not only an individual process, but also a relational one.

Open Dialogue: Regular, open, and honest communication is key when dealing with changes. Have conversations about how things are evolving and how it's affecting both parties involved. These discussions can be difficult, but they are essential for understanding and addressing any concerns or issues that arise.

Patience and Empathy: It's important to remember that changes impact everyone differently. What may seem like a small adjustment to you could be a significant shift for another. Be patient and empathetic towards others' feelings and perspectives as they, too, navigate through these changes.

Focus on Shared Interests: Even if changes lead to different lifestyles or viewpoints, it's crucial to remember what connected you in the first place. Maintaining shared interests or activities can provide a sense of stability and continuity amidst the changes.

Seek Professional Help if Needed: If changes in relationships lead to ongoing conflicts or feelings of distress, it may be beneficial to seek professional help.

Therapists and counselors can provide strategies to manage these changes effectively and healthily.

Handling changes in relationships is not always easy, but it is a necessary part of life. By approaching these shifts with understanding, openness, and a willingness to adapt, you can ensure that your relationships continue to be a source of support, comfort, and personal growth.

Finding and Joining Support Groups

There's an inherent strength in numbers. One of the most effective ways to bolster your support system is by becoming a part of a group whose members share your experiences, goals, or struggles. Support groups offer a unique blend of compassion, understanding, and practical advice that's hard to find elsewhere. In this section, we will explore the process of identifying, finding, and joining suitable support groups that can enhance your personal growth and resilience.

Identifying the Need for Additional Support

The first step in expanding your support network lies in recognizing that you need more help. It can be a challenging admission but remember that seeking support is not a sign of weakness, but rather a sign of strength.

This strength lies in your ability to understand your needs and take steps towards fulfilling them. Here's how you can identify if you need additional support:

Feeling Overwhelmed: If you find that you are regularly feeling overwhelmed, anxious, or depressed, and these feelings are not being adequately addressed within your existing support system, it might be time to seek additional help.

Crisis Points: Life throws curveballs—whether it's a significant life change, a loss, or a crisis, these events can push our coping mechanisms to their limits. If you're going through such an event, a support group can provide the much-needed assistance and understanding.

Isolation: Feelings of loneliness and isolation, despite having friends and family around, can indicate the need for more support. Support groups can offer a sense of community and belonging.

Desire to Connect: Sometimes, it's as simple as wanting to connect with people who understand your specific situation. This desire to be understood on a deeper level can be a strong indication of the need for a support group.

Remember, identifying the need is the first step towards finding the right help. This self-awareness is a sign of self-care, a necessary and critical part of maintaining mental and emotional health.

Locating Appropriate Support Groups

Once you've identified your need for additional support, the next step is to find the right group that can fulfill those needs. Locating the right support group involves careful research, and possibly some trial and error, but the benefits can be immensely rewarding. Let's look at some methods to locate appropriate support groups:

Internet Search: The internet is a vast resource when it comes to finding support groups. Use search engines to look for online forums, social media groups, and websites of organizations that cater to your need. Remember to use specific keywords related to your situation to narrow down the results.

Healthcare Providers: Healthcare professionals can be a rich source of information. Your doctor, therapist, or counselor likely has information about various support groups in your area or online. They can guide you towards groups that have been beneficial to their other patients.

Community Centers: Community centers often have information about local support groups. Libraries, religious centers, or even the local gym may have bulletin boards with flyers or posters for various support groups.

Friends and Family: Your existing support system may have suggestions for support groups that they know of or have heard good things about. Sometimes, the best recommendations come from people who know you well.

Workplace: Some workplaces offer employee assistance programs which may include support groups. Also, your HR department may have resources for locating support groups relevant to your situation.

When you have identified potential groups, do a bit of research on them. Look for reviews or testimonials and see if their meeting times and methods (online or in-person) fit your schedule and comfort level. Remember, the goal is to find a group where you feel comfortable, supported, and heard. It might take some time but finding the right group can be a transformative experience.

Participating and Engaging Effectively in These Groups

Once you've located an appropriate support group, the next important step is active participation. Effective engagement in a support group not only helps you, but also contributes to the overall strength and efficacy of the group.

Here are some suggestions to help you fully participate and engage:

Active Listening: Before you speak, listen. It's essential to be a good listener in a support group. When others share their experiences and feelings, listen attentively. Not only does this show respect, but you can learn a lot from the experiences of others.

Participation: After listening, participate actively. Share your experiences, thoughts, and feelings. Keep in mind that every person's contribution is unique and important. Remember, the more you put into the group, the more you will likely get out of it.

Be Respectful: Respect other people's perspectives, even if they differ from yours. A support group is a safe space for everyone, and each member must feel respected and valued. Avoid criticizing or making others feel uncomfortable with their experiences.

Keep Confidentiality: What is shared in the group should stay in the group. This is a key principle in all support groups and is essential for creating a safe and trusting environment.

Ask for Help: If you're struggling with something, ask the group for their thoughts and advice. They may offer different perspectives and solutions that you hadn't considered.

Consistency: Regular attendance and participation can help build and maintain momentum, for you and the group as a whole. Try to consistently attend meetings and contribute to the discussions.

By following these guidelines, you can help to create a positive, effective, and supportive environment for everyone. Remember, the goal of a support group is mutual aid - everyone is there to help and be helped, creating a powerful, shared journey of growth and healing.

Building a New Network of Like-Minded People

As life progresses, it's quite natural to encounter shifts in interests, goals, and values. This evolution of self can sometimes mean a change in the people we surround ourselves with. Building a new network of like-minded individuals can significantly enhance personal growth and be an excellent source of support, inspiration, and shared experiences.

The first crucial step in this process is identifying potential new social circles. These social circles can be a blend of individuals who share your passions, pursuits, or who are striving towards similar goals. The process of identification can be an exciting journey in and of itself. Be open to the opportunities that come your way and the people you encounter.

For instance, if you're enthusiastic about a specific hobby, you might find social circles in related clubs or online communities. Those passionate about fitness might find a supportive circle in a local gym or a yoga class. For book lovers, book clubs could offer a lively social circle with shared interests.

Similarly, if you're striving towards specific goals such as entrepreneurial success, joining a local business network, or even engaging with online forums for entrepreneurs can provide both friendships and valuable insight.

Remember, this process is about authenticity, finding individuals who align with your interests and aspirations. You're not just looking for any social circle, but the right one for you. In these circles, you'll find an exchange of ideas, shared experiences, and mutual support—making your journey more enjoyable and fruitful.

There's no rush in this process; it's not a race, but a personal journey. Each step you take towards finding your social circle is a step towards an enriched life, filled with meaningful connections.

By staying authentic to your interests and goals, you'll naturally gravitate towards like-minded people. Together, you can create a supportive environment, inspiring and encouraging each other towards personal growth and happiness.

Methods for Reaching Out and Connecting

Building a new network of like-minded individuals often hinges on the ability to reach out and initiate connections. Although it can be daunting, remember that every lasting relationship begins with a single interaction. Below are some strategies to make this process smoother and more successful.

Initiating Conversations: This is the first step towards making a connection. While it can feel challenging, starting a conversation is a powerful tool. It could be as simple as commenting on something shared in common or asking a question about the topic at hand. Remember, curiosity and genuine interest can be the best conversation starters.

Attending Events: Attend events that cater to your interests. This can be conferences, meet-ups, hobby clubs, or social gatherings. Participating in these events will increase your exposure to like-minded individuals, making the process of reaching out more natural.

Online Networking: The digital age has made it easier to connect with people worldwide who share similar interests. Social media platforms, online forums, and interest-based communities are excellent platforms for initiating contact and building relationships.

Volunteering: Contributing your time and effort to a cause you care about can connect you with individuals who share similar values. Volunteering not only helps build your social network but also offers a shared experience that can strengthen these relationships.

Be Open and Approachable: This goes beyond just wearing a welcoming smile. It's about your attitude and body language. Show genuine interest in others, maintain eye contact during conversations, and adopt an open posture. These signals show others that you're approachable and ready to connect.

Follow-up: Once you make an initial connection, ensure to follow up. You could send a friendly message or propose a meet-up, ensuring the relationship doesn't fade after the first encounter. Consistency is key in building and maintaining connections.

Each of these methods provides a pathway to connect with like-minded individuals. Remember, it's about quality, not quantity. Focus on building connections that offer mutual growth, respect, and support. Over time, these connections can turn into meaningful relationships that enrich your life and offer a robust support system.

Nurturing these New Relationships

When it comes to building and maintaining a network of like-minded individuals, merely making connections isn't enough. What's equally, if not more important, is nurturing these relationships. Establishing a deep and meaningful relationship with someone doesn't happen overnight. It requires effort, understanding, and time.

Start by showing interest in the other person's life and their passions. Learn about their background, their aspirations, and what motivates them. People often appreciate it when you take the time to understand them better.

During your conversations, listen attentively and provide thoughtful responses. Active listening not only shows that you care, but it also strengthens the bond between you and the other person.

Another key aspect of nurturing relationships is reliability. Be someone your connections can depend on. Whether it's meeting up when you said you would, keeping private conversations confidential, or delivering on a promise, showing that your dependable helps foster trust.

Also, consider how you can add value to their lives. Could you share a resource, offer a fresh perspective, or lend a helping hand? Adding value isn't about grand gestures; it's about how you can help each other grow.

Remember to maintain regular contact. This doesn't mean you need to be in touch daily, but don't let too much time pass without reaching out. It could be as simple as a message checking in on them or sharing something that you know they'd appreciate.

Lastly, be genuine. Authenticity forms the foundation of any strong relationship. People are more likely to reciprocate openness and form a meaningful connection when they sense genuineness from you.

In the end, the most meaningful relationships are those where both parties are invested, support each other, and value the connection.

The process may seem lengthy and require effort, but the result is a rich network of like-minded individuals that enrich your life in countless ways.

The key is to remain patient, and remember, the strength of your support system is not defined by the number of connections but the quality of those relationships.

Chapter 7: Rediscovering Your Identity

"New beginnings are often disguised as painful endings."

– Lao Tzu

One of the most common, yet damaging effects of divorce, is the loss of your sense of control. That is evident right from the beginning of the process. If divorce was not what you wanted, but nevertheless happened anyway, you will have experienced the loss of your sense of control at a higher level of magnitude.

If divorce was your choice, you will still struggle with a sense of control in many areas, but the decision to part ways was at least yours to make and you have had the dignity of choice. Having gone through the initial shock period of the separation, the ramifications quickly surface. Some of these can include finding a new place to live, relationships with in-laws now either severed or at risk, friendships potentially affected, especially if the friendships were forged during your time as a couple.

Others can be custody sharing arrangements, navigating through the severance of shared finances, and a sudden loss of identity.

Now add the next part of the process to the mix: The actual legal process of getting divorced. It's safe to say that most people have little or no experience with legal matters (except for less intrusive interactions, such as buying a house, having documents notarized, or having a will drawn up).

Our first interaction with the legal process of divorce can be intimidating and we are ill prepared for it. It can add uncertainty in a time of our lives where we already feel a lack of control and doubt.

It's around this time that you realize how much evidence and documentation you need just to get through the first part of the process. If you are highly organized and have kept meticulous records, this will make the process a little easier.

If not, you will be embarking on a journey to track down every receipt, income statement, pay stubs, income tax documents, bank and credit card statements, marital debt, pension funds, joint assets, and insurance information, just for starters. It cannot be stressed enough at this point: The sooner you collect these documents and submit them, the better.

The process of legal separation, between motions, statements of intent and court submissions can take months, even years.

At times, it feels like an endless tennis match where the ball keeps getting pinged back and forth between the two sides, not to mention the times in between when there is radio silence, and it doesn't seem like anything is happening.

You may lack control of the legal portion during this time, but you have full control over your attitude and outlook on life.

It is critical that you keep this in mind. Many become bitter and resentful during this process. This can have lasting negative effects that become a self-fulfilling prophecy.

Some people may see themselves as failures or with no future as a result. This can lead to self-destructive decision making, such as letting themselves go or no longer caring about their personal hygiene, for example.

We become who we think others want us to be. There are a lot of tools in the toolbox of self-destruction: Shame, inadequacy, little or no self-esteem, loneliness, irrational jealousy, not only feeling unloved but believing that no one can love us and, as a result, we will be alone forever. These are often triggered by memories of past rejection or abandonment.

We may react by using the only tools we know how to use. We've become experts in people-pleasing, where our mood depends on the mood of others. If they are happy, then we are happy. If they are angry or sad, we are angry or sad.

The only way for us to be happy again is to make the other person happy. We depend on others for mood approval and it's exhausting.

We spend time with people who bring out the worst in us and who are at times mean to us. We go out of our way to make ourselves available 24/7 in a desperate attempt to get others to like us, which of course has the opposite effect.

Others can see and smell the desperation and repel from us. We are in constant need of validation, so we may desperately try to create avatars on social media or pretend to live a life we don't actually live, so others can authorize our worthiness.

Remember that taking back control of your life starts with how you see yourself, not how you believe others may see you. Your belief in how others see you may be based on real or imagined perceptions.

Not only is it difficult to qualify those perceptions but you also have no control over them anyway. Seeing yourself as a hopeless failure because that's how you think others perceive you may lead you to make decisions that fulfill that description.

Maybe it's time to flip the script.

Ask yourself, are these people whose opinion you value anyway? What would happen if you disregarded what others thought of you and focused on how you see or feel about yourself?

It can be difficult to let go of how others perceive us. We may have inadvertently created our entire identity on how others perceive us and letting go now means we may not know who we are anymore.

Do it anyway. Let go. From the ashes we rise.

This isn't about creating a new identity but about reclaiming your original one. Who would you be if you stopped caring what others think? What would happen if you focused on you for a change?

In this thing we call life, there are moments of self-doubt, when we question the essence of our being. Who am I, we ask. Is this who I truly am, or is it a result of the numerous influences I have encountered? It is in these moments, we realize the need for introspection, to rediscover our identity.

Our identity isn't a fixed state of being. It is fluid, changing, and evolving as we move through life. Each experience, each person we meet, every book we read, all contribute to the shaping of our identity. It is a blend of nature and nurture, and the intricate interplay between the two is what molds us into the individuals we are.

As we navigate through the complexities of life, we often find ourselves lost. We wear numerous hats, conform to countless roles, and sometimes, in the process, we lose touch with our authentic selves. We get so engrossed in the act of fulfilling our responsibilities, that we forget to live for ourselves.

Self-discovery is a crucial part of self-growth. Understanding who we are, what we value, what we desire in life – these are essential aspects of our identity. These elements give us a sense of purpose, a direction to move forward. Rediscovering your identity may seem daunting. However, it is a rewarding journey that holds the promise of self-awareness and self-acceptance. It is about peeling back the layers of societal expectations, unmasking the facades we put on for the world, and reconnecting with our true selves.

Each one of us has a unique identity. It is this uniqueness that adds color and variety to the world. Embracing our identity, with all its facets, is not just about self-acceptance, but also about contributing our unique qualities to the greater good. There's no prescribed path to rediscovering your identity. It is a personal journey, filled with introspection, self-questioning, and realizations. You may have to confront your fears, challenge your beliefs, and step out of your comfort zone.

Rediscovering your identity is a step towards living a fulfilling and authentic life. It allows you to align your actions with your beliefs, desires, and values. It's a journey of understanding yourself, appreciating your individuality, and, most importantly, loving yourself.
Embrace the process, embrace the journey, and embark on a lifelong adventure of self-discovery and self-growth. The rediscovery of your identity is the first step in becoming the best version of yourself. Remember, it's not about changing who you are, but uncovering the real you, you that's been there all along.

Stay true to yourself, and the world will follow.

Reconnecting with Your Passions and Interests

We all have interests and passions that spark joy and breathe life into our existence. But as we grow older, the demands of life often push these passions to the back burner. We become so entwined with the responsibilities of our roles - as parents, as professionals, as community members - that we sometimes neglect our own interests. This section will help you reconnect with your passions and interests, an essential part of rediscovering your identity.

Rediscovering your passions starts with self-reflection. Think back to the times when you felt genuinely happy and excited. What were you doing? Maybe you loved painting as a child, but as an adult, you barely have time to pick up a brush.

Or maybe you used to spend hours in the kitchen experimenting with different cuisines, but now, cooking has been reduced to a mere survival skill. These activities are not just hobbies; they are reflections of your true self.

Once you have identified your past passions, the next step is to understand why you moved away from them. Was it due to lack of time?

Or perhaps you had to prioritize your career or family needs over your interests?

Understanding the 'why' can help you develop a plan to overcome these hurdles and reintegrate these passions into your life.

Reconnecting with your interests is not about radical changes, but more about subtle shifts in your lifestyle and mindset. It could be as simple as carving out half an hour every day to read, draw, garden, or whatever it is that you love. You might need to rearrange your schedule a bit or delegate certain tasks, but the joy and fulfillment you'll experience would be worth the effort.

Also, it's never too late to explore new interests. Stay curious and open-minded. Enroll in that photography course you always wanted to or join a book club. New experiences broaden your horizons and enrich your sense of self.

Reconnecting with your passions and interests is a significant part of rediscovering your identity. It is about aligning your life with what truly matters to you. And remember, these passions need not be grand or extraordinary. They are valuable because they bring you joy, rejuvenate your spirit, and make you, you.

So, take the leap, reignite your old passions, and explore new interests. Rekindle the spark within you and experience the fulfillment of living a life that resonates with your true self. Let your passions guide your journey to rediscovering your identity. After all, you are what you love.

Self-Reflection Exercises to Identify Your Interests

Identifying your true interests can be a transformative process. It can lead you towards a deeper understanding of who you are and what truly inspires you. Here are some exercises to guide you in this journey of self-discovery.

The Memory Lane Exercise: Make a list of activities you enjoyed doing as a child. Children are generally uninhibited by societal expectations or practical considerations, so this exercise can reveal your purest passions. As you note down these activities, try to remember how you felt when you were engaged in them. This exercise might stir up feelings of nostalgia, but it also holds the potential to revive forgotten passions.

The Joy List: Take a moment to think about activities that make you lose track of time. These are activities that you engage in not out of obligation or necessity but because they bring you genuine joy. Such activities can provide valuable clues about your true interests.

The Dream Scenario Exercise: Close your eyes and imagine you have an entire day free with no responsibilities or limitations. What would you choose to do? How would you spend this day? The answers to these questions can point towards activities that you wish you had more time for, providing insight into your passions.

The Strengths Finder: Reflect on your skills and strengths. What are you good at? Often, our interests align with our abilities. Recognizing these strengths can help you identify potential areas of interest.

The New Adventure: Finally, don't forget to consider new interests. Is there something you've always wanted to try but haven't gotten around to?
This might be a foreign language class, a cooking course, or a hiking expedition. By stepping out of your comfort zone and exploring new arenas, you might discover interests you never knew you had.

Engage in these self-reflection exercises honestly and patiently. Remember, this isn't a race; it's a journey towards understanding your true self. You might be surprised at what you discover. The insights gained from these exercises can serve as a steppingstone towards reigniting old passions and exploring new interests. Happy self-discovery!

Incorporating Your Passions into Your Daily Routine

Creating space for your passions in your daily routine is crucial for maintaining a sense of fulfillment and purpose in life. Here are a few strategies to help you seamlessly integrate your interests into everyday life.

Start Your Day with a Passion Project: Begin your day by spending some time on an activity you love. This could be reading, painting, exercising, or even gardening. Doing so can start your day on a positive note and set the tone for the rest of the day.

Use Lunch Breaks Wisely: Make the most of your breaks. Instead of mindlessly scrolling through social media or catching up on the news, you could dedicate this time to your interests. Read a book, write in your journal, or even practice a new language.

Integrate Interests with Tasks: Look for ways to incorporate your passions into your existing tasks. Love music? Listen to it while working. Passionate about cooking? Experiment with new recipes for dinner. This strategy can make mundane tasks more enjoyable.

Schedule 'Me' Time: Make sure to block off some time for yourself every day. Use this time to focus solely on your interests. Whether it's a half-hour of yoga or an hour of sketching, make it a non-negotiable part of your routine.

Use Technology to Your Advantage: There are numerous apps and platforms that can help you pursue your interests. If you're interested in learning a new language, apps like Duolingo can be beneficial. Or, if you're a book lover, you might find Audible or Kindle helpful for accessing books on the go.

Start Small and Be Consistent: Don't overwhelm yourself by trying to do too much at once. Start by incorporating small chunks of time for your interests and gradually increase it. Consistency is key in this process.

Connect with Like-Minded Individuals: Join clubs or online communities that share your interests. This can provide additional motivation to pursue your passions and could also lead to valuable friendships.

Integrating your passions into your daily routine is an ongoing process, and it requires patience and persistence. Yet, the rewards are significant, leading to a richer, more vibrant life. So, take the plunge and start infusing your day with the activities you love.

Embracing Self-Reflection and Personal Growth

Ah, self-reflection and personal growth, the inseparable twins of the self-improvement world! The only difference between the two is that self-reflection is the voice in your head saying, "Hey, are we doing, okay?" and personal growth is the voice in your head replying, "Not yet, but we're getting there."

To get this dialogue started, it's crucial to understand that self-reflection isn't something that happens when you're pondering life's mysteries in the shower or admiring the existentialism of a perfectly made latte. No, self-reflection is about looking at yourself honestly, even when the mirror says, "Honey, that shirt doesn't match those pants," or "Did you seriously think that karaoke performance of 'Bohemian Rhapsody' was a good idea?"

Once you've learned to accept the good, the bad, and the awkward about yourself, you can then start the exciting journey of personal growth. Picture it as a trip without a destination, where the real excitement is the journey itself.

And let's not forget, personal growth isn't like buying a bag of chips from the vending machine; it's more like a 'buy one, get ten free' deal. Improving one area of your life often has a ripple effect on other areas too.

You might wonder, "how can I grow if I keep making the same mistakes?" Well, making mistakes is like stepping on a banana peel in a comedy skit; it's funny, memorable, and you learn to avoid banana peels for the rest of your life. Remember, it's not about avoiding failure; it's about learning, adapting, and growing from it.

The wonderful thing about personal growth is that it's like climbing a hill where you can enjoy the view, see how far you've come, and get a clear vision of where you're going.

So, embrace self-reflection, don your hiking boots of personal growth, and start climbing. Just remember to enjoy the view along the way and, most importantly, don't step on any banana peels!

Understanding the Role of Introspection Post-Divorce

Divorce can feel like someone tossed your life in a blender and pushed 'puree.' You're suddenly split into a million little pieces, and while the blender's still whirring, you're trying to piece yourself back together. Now, that's where introspection steps in, with its tiny broom and dustpan, ready to help.

Let's be honest, introspection after a divorce is like deciding to do a deep clean of your house after a wild party; it's not the most fun task, but it's necessary. And just like cleaning up after the party, introspection isn't about finding who spilled wine on the couch or who broke your favorite lamp. It's about assessing the aftermath, picking up the pieces, and deciding what you want to keep and what you want to throw away.

Are you clinging onto habits or routines that no longer serve you? Maybe it's time to toss them out. Do you see qualities in yourself that you admire and want to develop further? Well, polish those up and put them on display. What about those sneaky, unnoticed parts of you that were quiet but supportive, like the book that props up the wobbly table or the coaster that protects the wooden surface from a hot cup? It's time to recognize and appreciate them too.

The great thing about introspection post-divorce is that it's a one-person show, with you as the lead actor, director, and audience. It's your chance to write your script, decide your narrative, and most importantly, give yourself a standing ovation.

So, dive into the sometimes-messy, sometimes-confusing, but always enlightening world of introspection. Take it one room at a time, one piece at a time, until you've reconstructed a life that reflects who you truly are. And remember, it's okay to laugh at the absurdity of it all; sometimes, laughter is the best cleaning agent.

Because if there's anything we've learned from late-night infomercials, it's that the best cleaning agents are the ones that can handle the toughest stains with a smile.
So why not approach introspection the same way? It's like those special sponges that claim to erase any mistake with just a bit of water - except your sponge is your sense of humor, and the water is your resilience.

When you're sorting through the clutter of emotions, thoughts, and memories that come with a divorce, it's all too easy to get lost in the chaos. It's like finding an old photo album in your attic, dusting it off, and suddenly getting caught in a whirlwind of nostalgia, regret, and 'what if' scenarios. But here's where you can sprinkle in a dash of humor.

Remember that time when you tried to bake a soufflé and it collapsed? Or that time when you both got lost on a road trip and ended up having the best time in a town you can't even pronounce?

Those moments are precious, not because they were perfect, but because they were uniquely yours.

Humor allows you to look at these moments and smile, to acknowledge the good times and the lessons learned. It allows you to accept your past without it being a burden, making the task of introspection less daunting.

The role of introspection post-divorce isn't to pull you back into the past but to guide you forward into your future. It's like using a GPS - you enter your starting point, not to stay there, but to figure out how to get to your destination. And just like a GPS, there will be many routes available, some will be quick, others scenic, and a few might have too many roundabouts. But ultimately, the choice is yours. Through introspection, you can decide which route you want to take, what speed you want to travel at, and what stops you want to make along the way.

So, buckle up, start your engine, and get ready for the journey of self-discovery. And remember, if you hit a speed bump or make a wrong turn, you can always reroute. Just keep your sense of humor handy, and you'll navigate the road of introspection like a pro.

Tools for effective self-reflection

Just as a handyman needs a toolbox to get a job done, so too do you need tools for the task of self-reflection. But don't worry, you won't need a hammer or a power drill for this task.

What you'll need are some metaphorical tools - patience, honesty, an open mind, and maybe a notebook to jot down your thoughts.

Let's start with patience. Self-reflection is not a one-time event. It's a process, an ongoing conversation with yourself. Imagine you're watching your favorite TV series, but you're trying to do it all in one day. By episode 10, you're bound to lose track of what's happening. Same goes for self-reflection. It's important to pace yourself and allow the process to unfold naturally.

Next, honesty. This tool is crucial in self-reflection. It's like your personal lie detector. It's about being truthful to yourself about your feelings, your actions, and their consequences.

Remember, you can't fool yourself. If you try, you're just wasting your time. And remember, honesty is the best policy, even when you're the only one in the room.

An open mind is also a key tool in your self-reflection toolkit. It allows you to see things from different perspectives, to challenge your own beliefs and assumptions. It's like wearing those multi-focal glasses - suddenly, you're able to see things that were outside your field of vision. So, keep your mind open and be ready to embrace new ideas and insights.

Lastly, a notebook or journal can be a practical tool for self-reflection. It provides a space where you can articulate your thoughts, feelings, and observations. It's like having a conversation with your future self. You can ask questions, make comments, even disagree with yourself. Plus, it has the bonus of being a great listener - it won't interrupt you or give unsolicited advice.

These tools for effective self-reflection can help you navigate the complexities of your inner world, allowing you to understand yourself better and gain clarity on your path forward.

So, grab your toolkit and get ready to dive into the fascinating journey of self-discovery. Remember, the only wrong way to use these tools is not to use them at all!

Cultivating Self-Confidence and Self-Worth

Picture this: You're standing in a garden, a garden that symbolizes your self-confidence and self-worth. But this garden has been neglected for a while. Weeds of self-doubt have sprouted, choking the beautiful blooms of self-esteem. It's high time to grab those gardening gloves and start the revitalization process.

Self-confidence and self-worth, like a garden, require time, attention, and care. They aren't things that suddenly blossom overnight, especially after enduring a hardship like a divorce.

But with a bit of persistence and nurturing, you can foster a garden brimming with self-assurance and a strong sense of self-worth.

Overcoming Self-Doubt and Rebuilding Self-Esteem

Let's say, hypothetically, you have a pesky weed in your garden. This weed is what we call self-doubt.

It's rather insistent, sprouting up when you least expect it, and often when you least need it. And like the weeds in your garden, self-doubt feeds off your energy and grows stronger, stifling the growth of your self-esteem blooms.

Self-doubt is like that troublesome garden gnome that pops up in the middle of your roses, diverting attention away from the beauty of the flowers to its unsettling smirk. You wonder, "How on earth did it get there? Who placed it right in the middle of my rose bushes?"

Metaphors aside, overcoming self-doubt is a process, and one that requires you to be as persistent as those weeds or that gnome. It demands that you continually pull-out self-deprecating thoughts from their roots and replace them with seeds of self-affirmation.

It requires you to remind yourself, time and again, that you are capable, you are worthy, and most importantly, you are more than your past relationships.

Rebuilding self-esteem is like tending to a garden post-weed-invasion. It's a gradual process, nurturing the soil of your mind, sowing the seeds of self-love, and watering them daily with affirmations and positive self-talk.
The fruits of this labor won't appear instantly, but with patience, you will see the buds of self-esteem sprout and eventually flower. So, put on your gardening gloves, and let's get to work. The garden of your self-confidence and self-worth is ready for its makeover.

Activities and exercises to foster self-confidence

Remember the garden metaphor? Think of these activities and exercises as your gardening tools - the spades, pruning shears, and watering cans - all geared towards helping you foster self-confidence.

Start a self-confidence journal: Here's the first tool in your gardening kit. In this journal, jot down your daily achievements, no matter how small.

Did you make your bed? That's an achievement! Did you finish a book? Kudos! This isn't about winning Nobel prizes. It's about recognizing that every step you take is a testament to your resilience and determination.

Explore new hobbies: This might sound like rearranging the flower beds in your garden for the fun of it but trying out new hobbies can help you discover new skills and talents. Whether it's knitting, salsa dancing, or deep-sea diving, the key here is to engage in activities that you enjoy and that make you feel accomplished.

Embrace self-care: Self-care activities are like adding a layer of mulch to your garden. They protect your newfound confidence by reducing stress and promoting feelings of wellbeing.

Whether it's a pampering spa day, a long walk-in nature, or indulging in your favorite book, find what makes you happy and incorporate it into your routine.

Affirmations and visualization: These are your sun and water for your self-confidence garden. Regularly practicing positive affirmations and visualizing your success can significantly enhance your self-confidence over time. Visualize your garden in full bloom - that's the power of positive thinking!

These activities aren't miracle cures. They are tools to assist you in your journey to cultivating self-confidence. It's a process that requires patience, care, and most importantly, a commitment to nurturing your self-worth. So, grab your gardening tools and start planting!

Developing a positive and self-affirming mindset

In the adventure of rediscovering your identity, developing a positive and self-affirming mindset is like finding the treasure map. It's the guide you need to navigate through the winding paths and dark forests of self-doubt and insecurity.

And don't worry, you won't need an old, cryptic parchment or a magical compass. All you need is tucked safely within you - your mindset.

Let's begin with a dose of humor. Imagine you're in a James Bond movie, surrounded by self-doubt henchmen. You need a secret weapon to get through, right? Well, that secret weapon is your mindset. Each time a henchman approaches, you whip out your positive thinking, like a secret gadget, and zap! The henchman disappears! Now, isn't that a much better visual than a dull, dreary fight with self-doubt?

But how does one cultivate this mindset? It starts with realizing that your thoughts shape your reality. Consider the glass half full or half empty debate. Depending on your perspective, you could be either sipping on optimism or drowning in pessimism. So, let's swap out the half-empty glass for a half-full one, and while we're at it, why not a full one? Now that's a refill of optimism!

You also need to embrace the power of affirmations. Think of them as your personal cheerleading squad, always ready to rally and root for you.

Start each day with a simple affirmation like "I am confident," or "I embrace my strengths." Remember, you are what you think.

This isn't about ignoring life's problems or hardships; it's about choosing to focus on the positive aspects and possibilities. So, let's jump off the pessimism train and board the optimism express. Remember, your mindset is your treasure map to rediscovering your identity. With the right mindset, the path to self-confidence and self-worth becomes an adventurous journey rather than a strenuous uphill climb. After all, who wouldn't prefer a treasure hunt over mountain trekking?

With a sprightly step, you take a leap from the pessimism train, leaving behind the echoing, somber horn, and the smoky trails of self-doubt. You land, almost heroically, onto the optimism express. As the train begins its journey, the landscape outside your window starts changing. There are still mountains to scale, but now they are covered in lush greenery and a halo of mist at the peak - much more inviting than before. The path uphill doesn't seem strenuous anymore. In fact, it's invigorating, filled with opportunities to bask in the mesmerizing views that only the heights can offer.

Remember, rediscovering your identity is not just about reaching the summit. It's also about the journey - the wind in your hair, the soft earth beneath your feet, the verdant canopy above you. It's about the thrill of encountering a rushing stream and the tranquility of discovering a tranquil glade. It's about enjoying the company of fellow travelers, some who join you for a brief while, and others who stick by your side for the long haul.

So, rather than treating the uphill climb as an ordeal, consider it an adventure. Each step you take is a step closer to rediscovering your authentic self. Each stumble and fall is a lesson, teaching you resilience and fortitude. And when you finally reach the summit, oh, the view is worth every bit of the journey!

Now, you might be wondering - how can we maintain this positive and self-affirming mindset amidst the everyday hustle and bustle? Well, the answer lies in daily practice.

Incorporate positive thinking into your daily routine. Start your day by counting your blessings, no matter how small. From the warmth of the morning sun to the refreshing sip of your favorite tea, each blessing is a reminder of the goodness in your life.

At the end of each day, jot down your achievements, again, no matter how small. Did you smile at a stranger? Jot it down. Did you finish a work project? Jot it down. Did you manage to do five minutes of meditation? Jot that down too. As you fill the pages with your achievements, you'll realize that you're more capable and worthy than you ever gave yourself credit for.

In the grand journey of rediscovery, maintaining a positive and self-affirming mindset is like ensuring your compass is well-calibrated. It keeps you focused on your path, wards off distractions, and guides you towards your true self. And remember, on this journey, you're not alone. You've got the best companion - yourself. With your positive mindset leading the way, you're bound to find the treasure you've been seeking - your identity.

Chapter 8: Exploring New Opportunities and Hobbies

"You can't go back and change the beginning, but you can start where you are and change the ending."
– C.S. Lewis

Remember that friend who, after a break-up, discovered they had a hidden talent for cooking? Or the co-worker who picked up salsa dancing to fill in the void of a failed relationship? These stories are more common than you might think, and they all pivot on one crucial ingredient – new opportunities and hobbies.

There's a bittersweet freedom that comes with divorce. You suddenly find yourself with all this unallocated time and space. Initially, it might seem overwhelming. You might feel an emptiness that you don't know how to fill. But consider this moment as a canvas. It's blank, sure, but that only means you have the full freedom to paint whatever you want on it.

Let's view this chapter of your life as a time of self-discovery and exploration. It's time to dive deep into yourself and discover what really lights you up. Remember, hobbies are not just pastimes. They are powerful tools for healing. They can offer a sense of achievement, create social connections, and provide a much-needed respite from the realities of life.

Broadening your Horizons through New Experiences

We often hear the phrase "life begins at the end of your comfort zone". While this might seem a bit cliché, it holds a kernel of truth. Broadening your horizons and stepping into the unfamiliar can lead to profound personal growth and unexpected joy. It's the call of the unknown that can inject fresh energy into our lives, and the aftermath of a divorce might be the perfect time to heed that call.

Venturing into New Interests: You might have a long-lost passion tucked away in the corners of your heart, or perhaps there's something you've always admired but never tried. This could be an art form, a new sport, or a language from a country you've always dreamed of visiting.

Now's the time to pick up that paintbrush, dust off those running shoes, or crack open that language guide. There are no rules here, only what brings you happiness and fulfillment.

Setting Achievable Goals: Having a new interest is exciting, but setting attainable goals is equally essential. This isn't about putting pressure on yourself; it's about marking progress. If you're getting into fitness, start with a 15-minute workout routine. If it's painting, complete one small canvas. The goal is to enjoy the journey while witnessing your own growth.

Taking Advantage of Online Resources: We live in the era of the internet, and countless resources are available at the tip of your fingers. From online courses to tutorials, blogs to forums, there's a wealth of information to guide you on your new path. Harness these resources and remember, it's okay to ask for help when you're learning something new.

Finding Comfort in the Unfamiliar: Remember, the unfamiliar may feel a bit uncomfortable at first, but that's where growth happens. Embrace it.

It might be a new language that tangles your tongue, a sport that challenges your endurance, or a hobby that demands patience.

It's all part of the journey, so don't rush it. Be gentle with yourself. Celebrate small victories and remember, it's about the experience, not just the end result.

Creating New Social Connections: As you explore your newfound interests, you're likely to cross paths with others who share your passions. This is a perfect opportunity to form new social connections. You might join a local group or club, participate in online forums, or even attend events related to your hobby. These connections can be a valuable source of support and friendship.

Meeting Like-minded Individuals: There's something incredibly rewarding about engaging with people who share your interests. Conversations come easy, and you find a common language in your shared passion. You might be surprised at how quickly bonds can form in these environments, and how these relationships can enrich your life.

Building a Supportive Network: Not only can these connections provide a sense of camaraderie, but they can also build a supportive network.

Everyone has their highs and lows, and having friends who understand your interests and challenges can be a great comfort. They can offer advice, share experiences, and provide the encouragement you need to keep going.

Engaging in Collaborative Learning: Exploring your hobby with others allows for collaborative learning. There's always something new to discover, and everyone brings unique insights to the table. You'll find that the exchange of knowledge is often a two-way street, offering an enriching and dynamic learning experience.

Finding a Sense of Belonging: Perhaps one of the most significant aspects of creating new social connections is the sense of belonging it can instill. As humans, we crave connections and community. By finding people who share your interests, you're cultivating your own community - one where you feel understood, supported, and valued.

Exploring new opportunities and hobbies after a significant life change like a divorce can feel overwhelming at first. But as you venture out, you'll find that this journey can be exciting, rewarding, and even therapeutic. In the process, you'll not only discover new interests, but also a new, enriching community that supports your personal growth.

Choosing learning opportunities that enhance your life, ah! Now we're getting to the fun part.

Let's set the scene: you're standing in front of a grand buffet of learning opportunities. They're all looking scrumptious - some seem exciting, some challenging, and a few downright peculiar. If this were an actual buffet, we'd have no issue - you'd have a taste of everything. But alas, this isn't about food. This is about time and energy. And unless you've discovered some secret fountain of eternal energy or mastered the art of time travel (if so, please share), you'll have to make choices.

First off, remember there's no need to approach this buffet like a starving person. Breathe. Take it slow. You don't have to dive headfirst into quantum physics or embark on learning the entire Mandarin language, not unless you really want to. Remember, this isn't a race. And even if it were, the race is against no one but yourself.

So, how to pick the right opportunities? Well, a little self-reflection goes a long way. Ask yourself, "Will this enhance my life in some way?" And I'm not talking about the grand, "this-will-transform-my-life" type of enhancement, though if it does, excellent. I'm referring to even the small ways – like learning to knit so you won't have to spend a small fortune on scarves every winter. Or taking a basic car maintenance course so you don't have to panic the next time your engine light starts blinking like a disco ball.

Consider the balance as well. A dash of practicality here, a pinch of passion there, perhaps a sprinkle of something challenging, just to spice things up a bit. You don't want to overload your plate with heavy, daunting tasks.

That's the equivalent of going for the stodgy mashed potatoes, mac n cheese, and a triple cheese pizza at the buffet. It's too much! Mix it up with something lighter and more enjoyable too.

Also, it's okay to sample. It's okay to dabble. If something's not to your taste, feel free to push it aside. Not every learning opportunity has to end with you being an expert. Sometimes, the experience is just about the journey.

And remember, it's your plate. You don't have to justify your choices to anyone else. If you want to learn juggling instead of Japanese, go for it! As long as you're enjoying the process and it brings value to your life in some way, it's worth pursuing.

Now, if you're anything like me, you might be worrying about picking the 'right' learning opportunity. We've all been there - it's like standing in front of an ice cream van on a hot day, trying to decide whether to go for a good old vanilla cone or be adventurous and try the new salted caramel flavor.

It's tough, right? But here's a little secret: there's no such thing as a 'wrong' choice here.

No, really. Every learning experience, whether it's learning to juggle, taking up Japanese, or even mastering the art of baking sourdough bread (trust me, it's an art), will add to your life in its own unique way. It might not always be in the way you expected, but that's the beauty of it. Just like you might surprise yourself by liking the salted caramel more than the vanilla.

You see, every new thing you learn is like adding a new tool to your life toolbox. And you never know when that tool might come in handy. Perhaps that juggling could be an icebreaker at a party.

Or maybe, that Japanese could help you connect with a new friend or decipher the instructions on that gadget you ordered online. And let's not even get started on the glory of freshly baked sourdough bread.

Remember, the goal isn't always about being the best, getting recognition, or achieving some sort of tangible reward. The beauty of exploring new opportunities and hobbies lies in the joy of the process, the thrill of discovery, and the satisfaction of seeing yourself grow and evolve.

Also, never forget that you're not on any sort of deadline. Learning is not a race, and you don't get bonus points for finishing first. You're allowed to take your time, go at your own pace, and choose your own path. And if you ever stumble or lose your way, that's okay too. You're allowed to pick yourself up, dust yourself off, and either continue from where you left off or choose a whole new direction.

So be bold and curious. Be ready to embrace the unfamiliar and step outside your comfort zone. Don't be afraid of making 'mistakes,' because in the grand adventure of learning, there are no mistakes, only lessons.

Now, let's get out there and start exploring! Let's live and learn, laugh and grow. And let's make our lives richer and more interesting with every new experience we embrace. Remember, the world is your buffet. Enjoy!

The Value of Stepping Outside of Your Comfort Zone

Alright, let's get real for a minute. You know that warm, cozy feeling you get when you're snuggled up in your favorite blanket, sipping on a hot cup of cocoa, watching your favorite TV show?

That's your comfort zone. It's familiar, it's safe, and it's easy. But what if I told you that there's a whole world out there, waiting for you to explore, just beyond that comfort blanket?

Now, I know what you're thinking. Why would I want to leave my comfort zone? It's comfortable! And you're right. It is. But, here's the thing: real growth, the kind that makes you stretch and strive, that makes you learn and evolve, that kind doesn't happen in the cozy confines of your comfort zone.

It happens when you dare to step outside, when you dare to challenge yourself and take on something new and unfamiliar.

Imagine for a moment you're a seed. Safe and warm in your little shell, tucked away under the soil. It's nice in there, isn't it? But if you remain a seed, that's all you'll ever be. To become a tree, to grow and bloom, you have to push through the soil, reach for the sun, brave the winds and the rains. Only then can you truly flourish.

So, what does step outside of your comfort zone look like? It could be anything. Maybe it's signing up for a cooking class, even though you've never so much as scrambled an egg before.

Maybe it's joining a local sports team, despite feeling a bit out of shape. Or perhaps it's learning to dance, even if you've got two left feet. The point is it doesn't matter what you choose. What matters is that you're choosing to challenge yourself. You're choosing growth over comfort.

Because each time you step outside your comfort zone, you're not just learning a new skill or hobby. You're learning about yourself. You're learning that you're stronger than you thought, braver than you believed, and capable of so much more than you imagined.

Of course, it's not going to be easy. There will be moments of frustration, doubt, and even failure. But remember, each stumble, each fall, it's not a setback. It's a steppingstone. It's a lesson learned, a hurdle overcome, a testament to your courage and determination.

So, take that leap. Step outside your comfort zone. Yes, it might be scary. Yes, it might be challenging. But it will also be exhilarating, empowering, and oh-so rewarding. Because, that's where the magic happens. That's where you truly start to live, to grow, to shine. And I promise you, it's worth every bit of effort.

Identifying Opportunities for New Experiences

Picture yourself standing on a vast beach, staring out into an endless horizon of possibilities.

The sheer potential for new experiences is as wide and as deep as the ocean before you. It may seem overwhelming at first, but once you start seeing the opportunities for what they are - chances to grow, learn, and discover - that vast ocean becomes a playground of potential. Now, let's dive in and figure out how we can spot these wonderful opportunities for new experiences.

Listen to Your Curiosity

Your curiosity is like a built-in compass, pointing you towards things that spark your interest. Often, we silence this voice, dismissing it as impractical or irrelevant. But if we start paying attention, our curiosity can lead us to new hobbies, interesting knowledge, and fulfilling experiences.

Whether it's an intriguing book title, an interesting podcast topic, or an unusual hobby you heard about in a casual conversation, let your curiosity guide you. And once it does, don't hesitate to explore it further.

Keep an Open Mind

Keeping an open mind is like having a wide-angle lens on your life. It allows you to see more, perceive more, and ultimately, experience more. When you're open to new ideas, new cultures, new perspectives, you're not just opening the door to new experiences, you're also cultivating a mindset that embraces change and growth. In practical terms, this might mean saying yes to trying new foods, attending different cultural events, or simply engaging in conversations with people who have different views and experiences than yours. You might be surprised how much you can learn and grow from these interactions.

Actively Seek Out New Experiences

This is the equivalent of getting off the tour bus and wandering down the backstreets. It's about actively looking for new opportunities rather than waiting for them to find you. This could be as simple as checking out that new museum exhibits you've been curious about or signing up for that pottery class you saw advertised in the local paper.

And, of course, this doesn't have to be limited to your local area. With the digital age, the world is literally at your fingertips. Online platforms offer countless opportunities to learn new skills, engage with different communities, and explore new ideas. So go ahead, sign up for that online course, join that digital book club, or even start your own blog.

Embrace the Unexpected

Opportunities for new experiences often come in unexpected forms and at unexpected times. Maybe it's an impromptu invitation to a salsa dance class or a sudden chance to try paragliding during a vacation.

Rather than shying away from these unexpected opportunities, embrace them. Even if the experience isn't something you typically see yourself doing, give it a try. You might find a new passion, meet interesting people, or simply have a good story to tell.

Reflect on Your Interests

Take some time to reflect on what interests and excites you. Maybe you've always been fascinated by the stars and the mysteries of the universe.

Why not turn this interest into an experience by learning more about astronomy or visiting a planetarium? Or perhaps you love the idea of being able to create your own clothes. Consider taking up sewing or fashion design. By aligning your new experiences with your interests, you'll not only enjoy the process more, but you're also more likely to stick with it in the long run.

Connecting the Dots

Let's talk about Steve Jobs for a minute. No, I'm not saying you have to start a tech empire or wear black turtlenecks every day. But there's something he said in a commencement speech that resonates deeply with our topic of discussion. He advised, "You can't connect the dots looking forward; you can only connect them looking backward. So, you have to trust that the dots will somehow connect in your future."

In essence, he was saying that every experience, every encounter, every newly acquired piece of knowledge or skill is like a dot. At the time, you may not see how it fits into the grand scheme of your life.

It may even seem random or irrelevant. But as time goes on and you gather more and more of these dots, patterns start to emerge. Interests evolve. Passions develop. Opportunities arise. And before you know it, these seemingly random dots start connecting in ways you could never have predicted.

Making Space for New Experiences

There's one more thing to consider when it comes to identifying opportunities for new experiences. And that is, quite simply, making space for them. Life can get busy. We get so caught up in our routines and responsibilities that we forget to leave room for novelty, for exploration, for growth. So, as much as it's about spotting the opportunities, it's also about creating the time and space to pursue them.

This doesn't necessarily mean you have to quit your job and travel the world (although, if that's what you want to do, power to you!). It could simply mean dedicating an hour each week to learning a new skill. Or setting aside one weekend a month to try something new. Or even just taking five minutes each day to read about a topic you're curious about. Small as these steps may seem, they can open up a world of opportunities for new experiences.

Identifying opportunities for new experiences is a dynamic process that involves curiosity, openness, active seeking, and a willingness to embrace the unexpected. It's about following your interests and passions, trusting that they will lead to valuable experiences and learnings. And, importantly, it's about making space in your life to explore these opportunities.

As you start to adopt this mindset and approach, you'll find that the world becomes a more exciting and stimulating place. You'll see opportunities where you didn't before, and you'll be more prepared to seize them when they arise. You're about to embark on a lifelong journey of discovery and growth, and I can't wait to see where it takes you.

Lifelong Learning as a Tool for Personal Growth

From the moment we open our eyes as infants, we start learning. And, if we're smart, we never stop. Lifelong learning is more than just education, it's about constantly growing, evolving, and becoming the best version of yourself.

Personal growth is a continuous journey that extends well beyond formal education, and it's something that we should all be excited about. It's a journey that is full of surprises, full of ups and downs, and most importantly, full of fun!

But why is lifelong learning such an important tool for personal growth? Well, let's start by looking at the very definition of personal growth. It involves the growth and enhancement of all aspects of the person, the feelings the person has about themselves, and their effectiveness in living.

It includes the development of positive life skills and the development of a realistic and healthy self-esteem. So, if we were to put it simply, personal growth equals learning. Now, let's not limit learning to just new skills or knowledge.

Learning also involves understanding our strengths and weaknesses, our passions, our values, and our beliefs. It's about understanding who we are and who we want to be. It's about knowing where we are and where we want to go. And it's about making a plan and taking action to get there.

This process of self-discovery and self-improvement can be both exciting and challenging. It's like a thrilling ride with unpredictable twists and turns. But with every challenge we overcome, every barrier we break, every fear we conquer, we grow. And with every step of growth, we become more confident, more resilient, and more capable.

With every new idea, every piece of knowledge we acquire, every new skill we hone, we are effectively expanding our horizons, and consequently, our self-confidence. Each new chapter of learning marks a chapter in the book of our personal growth and development. Learning becomes a journey of self-discovery, which in itself is an endlessly fascinating adventure, don't you agree?

When you learn something new, you're not just adding another feather to your cap, you're essentially adding a layer to your self-esteem. Just think about the surge of satisfaction and pride you feel when you get the hang of a particularly tough concept or successfully complete a challenging project. That's the power of learning at work.

However, learning isn't always about the big, monumental milestones. It's equally about appreciating the smaller steps, the seemingly insignificant progressions that accumulate over time to result in substantial growth. Remember when you first decided to start cooking, for instance?

You might not have whipped up a five-course meal on your first day. Maybe it was just a simple pasta dish, but hey, you made it yourself! That's something to be proud of, and it likely gave you the confidence to try out more complex recipes later.

Then there's the fun aspect. Learning keeps your brain active and engaged, and let's be honest, it's always entertaining to explore new topics or skills. You might laugh at your initial attempts, maybe even make a blooper or two, but that's all part of the process. Don't be afraid to laugh at yourself along the way; it's a sign that you're human and you're learning. And the journey becomes more enjoyable when you can look at it with a sense of humor and lightheartedness.

That being said, keep in mind that everyone's learning journey is different, just like every individual is unique. The pace, the method, the subject - it all depends on you. What matters most is that you remain dedicated to this path of continuous learning and growth. The rewards, in the form of boosted confidence and a heightened sense of self-worth, will certainly be worth it.

Choosing Learning Opportunities That Enhance Your Life

Take a moment to consider the countless learning opportunities that surround you each day. They might be hidden in the pages of a book, in the tranquility of nature, or in the hustle and bustle of the urban landscape. Sometimes, they're cloaked in the quiet wisdom of the elderly, or they might be hidden within a child's innocent question. Often, these opportunities are simply waiting for you to take the first step, reach out, and grasp them.

To truly enrich your life, it's crucial to carefully select these learning opportunities based on their potential to nurture your growth, broaden your perspectives, and contribute to your overall well-being. But how exactly do we do that?

Aligning with Your Goals: First things first, any learning opportunity you select should ideally align with your personal or professional goals. For instance, if you aim to improve your physical fitness, a yoga or dance class might be a perfect fit.

If you're planning a career change, maybe an online certification course would be the way to go. The key is to ensure that whatever you're learning brings you a step closer to your aspirations.

Feeding Your Curiosity: Never underestimate the power of curiosity! Are you intrigued by the mysteries of the universe, the human mind, or the underwater world? Well, then why not learn more about it?

Opt for opportunities that feed your sense of wonder and curiosity, as these are the ones that will keep you engaged and excited.

Promoting Personal Growth: Seek out learning opportunities that encourage you to grow as an individual. This could be anything from a book club that stimulates thoughtful discussions, a public speaking workshop to enhance your confidence, or a mindfulness retreat to promote inner peace.

Fostering Connections: Learning is often more enjoyable when it's a shared experience. Try to choose opportunities that allow you to connect with others - be it a cooking class, a foreign language group, or a community gardening project. Such engagements can provide a wonderful platform to learn, bond, and create lasting memories.

Staying Flexible and Open-Minded: Remember, it's okay to change your mind. If you discover that a particular learning opportunity isn't what you expected, don't be afraid to switch gears. Stay flexible, keep an open mind, and remember that every experience - even those that seem disappointing at first - can teach us something valuable.

So, there you have it - a simple guide to help you choose the learning opportunities that will truly enhance your life. It's a fascinating world out there, filled with knowledge and experiences just waiting to be explored. So go ahead, take that leap, and discover the joy of lifelong learning.

Leveraging Learning to Boost Confidence and Self-Worth

It's an exciting realization, isn't it? That every book you read, every new skill you acquire, every piece of knowledge you gain is more than just information. It's a powerful tool you can leverage to boost your confidence and self-worth. It's like discovering you've been carrying a magic wand all along, you just didn't know how to use it. So, let's figure out how to wield this power of learning, shall we?

Learning, when purposefully channeled, can indeed work wonders on your confidence. Remember the time when you finally got a handle on that tricky piece of software, or when you delivered your first speech in a foreign language? You could practically feel your confidence soaring, right?

That's the magic of learning. Each new concept you grasp, each challenge you overcome, every tiny win along your learning journey fuels your self-belief, reinforcing the idea that 'Yes, I can do this!'

And this is a feeling that transcends into all areas of your life.

In a similar vein, learning also elevates your self-worth. As you expand your knowledge base and skill set, you become increasingly valuable - to your team at work, to your family at home, and most importantly, to yourself. You begin to appreciate the vast potential that resides within you, an ever-expanding universe of capabilities and possibilities.

So how can you leverage learning to boost your confidence and self-worth?

Embrace Challenges: Step out of your comfort zone and take on tasks that stretch your abilities. Each time you overcome a challenge, it reinforces your belief in your abilities, enhancing your confidence.

Celebrate Wins: Don't wait for major accomplishments to pat yourself on the back. Celebrate small victories along your learning journey. Each win, no matter how small, is a testament to your progress and worth celebrating.

Engage in Continuous Learning: Make learning an ongoing process. By continually adding to your knowledge and skill set, you're not only making yourself more valuable, but you're also bolstering your confidence.

Acknowledge your Growth: Take a moment to reflect on what you've learned and how far you've come. This self-recognition boosts your self-worth and motivates you to keep moving forward.

Learning is more than just acquiring new information. It's about self-discovery, growth, and building a robust sense of self. So, keep learning, keep growing, and let your confidence and self-worth reach new heights.

Chapter 9: Embracing Your Newfound Happiness and Independence

"Everyone thinks of changing the world, but no one thinks of changing themself."

– Leo Tolstoy

Life is a journey, and while the path may be filled with bumps and turns, there is also beauty and growth in every step. In this part of the journey through divorce, it's time to take a moment and celebrate your progress. After all, you've braved the storm, walked through the darkness, and emerged stronger and more self-aware.

Recognizing and Celebrating Your Achievements

You have learned to accept the reality of your divorce, you have navigated your way through the turmoil of emotions and you have started rebuilding your life.

And lastly, you have begun to discover who you truly are outside of the context of your previous marriage. These are all significant milestones worth acknowledging.

Recognizing your achievements doesn’t require grand gestures. It begins with self-reflection. Take some time to sit down and consider the emotional distance you have traveled. How have you grown? What have you learned about yourself? What are the things that you are doing now that you couldn't do before?

Celebrate the resilience you've shown in facing this ordeal. Applaud yourself for the courage you've displayed in confronting your pain. Be proud of the strength you’ve found within yourself to rebuild your life after divorce.

In recognizing your achievements, remember that it's not just about the final outcome. It's about the steps you've taken, the difficulties you've overcome, the personal battles you've won, and the process you've undergone to get where you are now.

Whether it's finding peace in solitude, creating new traditions, setting and accomplishing new goals, or even establishing healthier relationships - every step towards growth and healing is a victory. Even small wins are still wins.

A powerful way to honor your progress is by journaling your journey. Writing your thoughts and feelings can provide a tangible record of your evolution. Over time, you will be amazed at how far you've come, and you will find inspiration in your own words.

You can also celebrate your achievements by treating yourself. It doesn't have to be lavish. It could be as simple as taking a day off to enjoy your favorite book or hobby, having a nice meal, or taking a short trip. Moreover, remember to share your victories with those close to you. Not only will it amplify your joy, but it can also provide encouragement for others who might be dealing with similar struggles.

As you celebrate your achievements, it is important to remember that you are not just surviving; you are thriving. You are rediscovering your own potential, embracing your independence, and experiencing a newfound happiness.

Importance of Acknowledging Your Progress

Acknowledging your progress is not just about celebrating your wins or stroking your ego. It's an essential component of your overall wellbeing and personal development, especially in the aftermath of a significant life event like divorce. Here's why acknowledging your progress is so crucial.

Promotes Self-Awareness: Taking time to acknowledge your progress encourages you to reflect on your journey. You become more self-aware as you notice patterns in your behavior, changes in your attitudes, and evolution in your thoughts and emotions.

Boosts Self-Confidence: Recognizing your achievements enhances your self-esteem and self-confidence. Each accomplishment, no matter how small, is proof of your capabilities and resilience. It reminds you of your strength and adaptability.

Motivates You: When you acknowledge your progress, you are essentially validating your efforts. This fuels your motivation to continue growing and working towards your goals. It offers a clear indication that you're moving forward, that change is happening, even if it's gradual.

Cultivates Positivity: Celebrating your wins, big and small, helps cultivate a positive mindset. It shifts your focus from what's going wrong to what's going right, encouraging an optimistic outlook on life.

Enhances Emotional Well-being: Progress recognition can provide a much-needed emotional boost. It can elicit feelings of pride, contentment, and fulfillment, which can contribute significantly to your overall happiness and satisfaction.

Encourages Persistence: Progress, especially in the realm of personal growth and healing, can be slow and sometimes invisible. By consciously acknowledging your progress, you remind yourself that you're on the right track. This can inspire you to stay persistent in the face of adversity and not give up.

Fosters Gratitude: Finally, acknowledging your progress can foster a sense of gratitude. As you reflect on your journey and recognize the strides you've made, you become more appreciative of your inner strength, the support you've received, and the lessons you've learned.

Acknowledging your progress is a simple yet profound way to embrace your journey. It empowers you to honor your resilience, cherish your growth, and acknowledge your evolution. It's a reminder that you're more than just a divorcee—you're a survivor, a warrior, and a beacon of strength and inspiration.

Strategies for Tracking and Celebrating Your Achievements

Acknowledging your progress and celebrating your achievements require a conscious effort. It's not always easy to see how far we've come, especially when we're still on the journey. Here are some strategies to help you track your progress and celebrate your achievements:

Maintain a Progress Journal: A journal dedicated to documenting your progress can be an effective tool. Write about your feelings, the challenges you overcame, the small victories you had each day, and the steps you took towards your goals. Not only does this act as a cathartic outlet, but it also creates a tangible record of your journey that you can reflect upon.

Set Clear Goals: Setting clear, measurable goals can help track your progress. Goals act as milestones on your journey, providing structure and a sense of direction. Celebrate every time you achieve a goal, no matter how small it may seem.

Regular Self-Reflection: Dedicate time regularly (weekly, monthly) to self-reflect on your progress. Ask yourself questions such as, "What did I learn this month?" "How have I grown?" "What have I achieved?" This can provide a clearer view of your journey and the progress you've made.

Use Visual Representation: Visuals can make progress more evident and gratifying. Use tools like progress bars, pie charts, or calendars to mark your milestones. These visual aids can give you a sense of accomplishment as you see your progress manifested physically.

Engage a Support Network: Share your victories with your support network - friends, family, or a support group. They can provide encouragement, share in your joy, and help validate your progress. They may also offer perspective that you might have missed.

Practice Gratitude: Regularly express gratitude for your achievements. This could be through a daily gratitude journal or quiet moments of thanks. Recognizing the good in your life can help maintain a positive outlook.

Reward Yourself: Finally, celebrate your achievements by rewarding yourself. This doesn't always mean extravagant gifts or treats. It could be as simple as giving yourself a day off, reading a book you love, taking a relaxing bath, or indulging in your favorite hobby.

By consciously tracking and celebrating your achievements, you cultivate a mindset that values progress and cherishes growth. This not only helps you appreciate the journey you've embarked upon but also encourages you to keep going, even when the path gets tough.

Overcoming the Habit of Self-Criticism and Focusing on Positives

You know, it's surprising how often we become our own harshest critics. It seems almost second nature to downplay our achievements and focus on our shortcomings instead.

"Sure, I may have completed that project ahead of schedule, but I could've done a better job on the presentation," or "I've started exercising regularly, but I'm still not losing as much weight as I'd like." Does that sound familiar? Don't worry, you're not alone in this. We've all been there, and it's this cycle of self-criticism that we need to break to truly embrace our newfound happiness and independence.

Let's imagine you're learning to cook. The first few attempts might not go as planned. The pasta could turn out too sticky, the sauce too runny. Now, it's easy to slip into the mode of "I'm a terrible cook." But wait, remember that you're just learning. It takes time to perfect any skill, doesn't it?

Instead of criticizing yourself, what if you said, "Well, the pasta didn't turn out perfect, but hey, I managed to make it edible on my first try. Plus, now I know what to watch out for next time." Sounds better, doesn't it? This is the power of focusing on the positives.

Now, this doesn't mean ignoring areas you can improve upon, but rather, shifting your focus from purely what's 'wrong' to also appreciating what's 'right'. And there are always positives to find if you look for them, just like in our cooking example.

One way to do this is by adopting a daily ritual of focusing on your achievements. At the end of each day, make a list of things you've accomplished, no matter how small they seem. This act of 'positive accounting' can help highlight the good parts of your day and foster a positive self-perception.

Another key element in overcoming self-criticism is self-compassion. We all make mistakes, we all have flaws, and that's okay. We need to give ourselves the same understanding and kindness we'd offer a friend. So next time you stumble, instead of berating yourself, try to comfort and reassure yourself. Say, "It's okay, everyone messes up sometimes. I'll try again and do better."

Remember, the goal here isn't to achieve perfection. It's to foster a kinder, more understanding relationship with yourself. It's to celebrate the progress you've made and the person you're becoming. So, here's to overcoming self-criticism, embracing the positives, and welcoming our newfound happiness and independence.

And so, as we continue on this journey towards self-discovery and independence, it's essential to remember to be patient with ourselves. No transformation happens overnight. Every small step forward is an achievement worth celebrating.

Just as a painter doesn't create a masterpiece in a single stroke, you won't achieve your goals all at once. Each brushstroke, each decision, each day, brings you closer to the person you want to become.

And just like that painter, it's important to step back now and then, assess your progress, and appreciate the masterpiece that is your life in the making.

Let's say you've decided to pick up a new language. You've been studying diligently for months, and one day, while watching a foreign film, you realize you understood a whole sentence without reading the subtitles. That's a great achievement! Instead of brushing it off as trivial or telling yourself, "But there's so much more I don't understand yet," take a moment to appreciate how far you've come.

The road to embracing our newfound happiness and independence isn't always smooth, but each bump, each detour is an opportunity for growth. It's in these moments, when we face challenges or make mistakes, that we learn the most about ourselves and our resilience.

Don't let these moments deter you. Instead, use them as steppingstones towards your goal. Every time you overcome an obstacle, take a moment to recognize your strength and courage. These small wins can be immensely empowering and will fuel your journey further.

Overcoming the habit of self-criticism and focusing on the positives is a crucial step towards embracing our newfound happiness and independence. By acknowledging our progress, celebrating our achievements, and being patient and compassionate with ourselves, we pave the way for a fulfilling and independent life. Remember, you are the author of your story. So, let's make it one of growth, resilience, and most importantly, happiness.

Cultivating Gratitude and Positivity

Let's take a minute and talk about something that can have a huge impact on our overall sense of happiness and independence: gratitude and positivity.

You know that feeling when you take a deep breath, look around, and just appreciate the fact that you're alive and part of this incredible world? That's what we're aiming for here, and let me tell you, it's a game-changer.

Benefits of a Gratitude-Oriented Mindset

Having a gratitude-oriented mindset or being consciously aware of all the good things in your life and expressing appreciation for them, can shift your perspective in such a way that life just looks and feels different, in the best possible way.

Picture this. You're stuck in traffic, which is irritating, to say the least, but instead of letting that frustration consume you, you switch on the radio. Your favorite song comes on, and in that moment, you decide to focus on the music, the lyrics, the joy that song brings you. You're practicing gratitude right there in your car, despite the bumper-to-bumper traffic. This small shift in perspective can transform an otherwise frustrating experience into a moment of joy and gratitude.

Having a gratitude-oriented mindset offers numerous benefits. For one, it helps in reducing stress and anxiety. By focusing on the positive aspects of life, we can combat the negativity that often leads to these feelings. This shift can also boost our resilience, enabling us to navigate through life's challenges with more grace and composure.

Another beautiful thing about gratitude is that it tends to encourage positive relationships. When we're able to see and appreciate the good in others, it helps foster stronger, more meaningful connections.

Plus, guess what? Gratitude can also improve our physical health. Yep, you heard right! Studies have shown that individuals who practice gratitude regularly tend to have lower blood pressure, improved immune function, and better sleep quality. Not bad for just saying 'thank you', right?

In short, a gratitude-oriented mindset not only boosts our happiness and positivity but also improves our overall well-being. So, are you ready to dive into the world of gratitude? It's a journey well worth taking.

Practices for Fostering Gratitude and Positivity

Now that you're familiar with all the incredible benefits of a gratitude-oriented mindset, you might be wondering, "That sounds great, but how exactly do I cultivate this in my daily life?"

Well, I'm glad you asked. Let's dive into some practical ways to foster gratitude and positivity.

First up, we have what I like to call a 'Gratitude Journal'. This is a simple yet powerful practice. All it takes is a few minutes at the start or end of your day to write down three things you're grateful for. These don't have to be monumental things.

Maybe you're grateful for the delicious cup of coffee you had this morning, or for the friend who sent you a funny meme that made you laugh. Over time, you'll start to notice all the little joys sprinkled throughout your day.

Another great practice is 'Gratitude Prompts'. This involves asking yourself questions that encourage a sense of appreciation. Questions like "What is something that made me smile today?" or "Who in my life am I thankful for and why?" The answers to these questions help you tap into feelings of gratitude that might otherwise go unnoticed.

Then we have what's known as a 'Gratitude Walk'. This is exactly what it sounds like. You take a walk - it could be around your neighborhood, a local park, or even just your backyard - and as you do, you intentionally look for things to be grateful for.

It could be the sound of birds singing, the feeling of the sun on your skin, or the sight of a beautiful flower. This exercise not only helps cultivate gratitude, but it also allows you to connect with nature and find peace in the present moment.

Finally, there's the practice of 'Gratitude Reminders'. These are little cues that you set up in your environment to remind you to pause and appreciate. It could be a sticky note on your mirror that says, "What are you grateful for today?" or an alarm on your phone that prompts you to pause and find something to appreciate.

These are just a few practices to help you foster gratitude and positivity. Remember, it's not about massive changes, but small, consistent practices that can make a big difference.

Just like muscles, your gratitude muscle needs regular exercise. So pick a practice or two, start flexing that gratitude muscle, and watch as your world starts to shift in beautiful, unexpected ways.

Overcoming Challenges and Setbacks with a Positive Outlook

The path to newfound happiness and independence isn't always smooth. Challenges and setbacks are part and parcel of life. But here's the thing - these hurdles do not define us; our reactions do. And while we can't always control what happens to us, we can control how we respond to it. This is where a positive outlook can be a game-changer.

When faced with a challenge, the initial reaction might be to focus on the negative, to dwell on the "why me?" But what if, instead, you chose to view this challenge as an opportunity? An opportunity to learn something new, to grow, to become more resilient. This shift in perspective can make a world of difference. It's like putting on a new pair of glasses that help you see your situation in a different light.

Let's take a practical example. Imagine you've had a falling out with a close friend. You might initially feel hurt, confused, even angry. But what if you chose to view this as an opportunity? An opportunity to better understand yourself and your needs in a friendship, to communicate more effectively, or to practice forgiveness. Suddenly, a difficult situation has transformed into a learning experience.

That's not to say it's easy. It takes practice. But remember, you've already made so much progress on your journey. You've overcome hurdles before, and you can do it again. And each time you do, you become stronger and more resilient.

Adopting a positive outlook also involves letting go of the idea of perfection. Life is messy and that's okay. Instead of striving for a flawless journey, aim for progress. Celebrate the small wins, the learning moments, the times you got back up after a fall.

Remember, it's okay to have bad days. It's okay to feel down sometimes. But don't let these moments define you. Instead, view them as opportunities to grow, to learn, and to continue on your journey with newfound strength and wisdom.

So, next time you face a challenge, take a deep breath, put on your positivity glasses, and remind yourself: "I got this. This is an opportunity for growth. I am resilient and I can overcome this." Because you can, and you will. After all, you've come this far, haven't you?

Envisioning a Brighter Future

And now, we take a step into the future. Yes, we're on this amazing journey, and we're becoming more independent and happier each day. But where are we headed? What does our destination look like? These are important questions to ask ourselves. And this is where goal setting comes into play.

The Role of Goal Setting in Shaping Your Future

Now, I know what you're thinking. Goal setting, huh? Been there, done that. And yes, we've all set goals in our lives. But we're going to approach it a little differently this time.

Goal setting is not just about writing down a list of things we want to achieve. It's more than just a roadmap. It's a tool that helps us shape our future. It's a way of telling ourselves, "This is where I want to be. This is the person I want to become."

And the beauty of goal setting? It's all in your hands. You're the one in control here. You're the one who decides what you want out of your life. Pretty empowering, right?

Consider it this way. Think about going on a trip. You wouldn't just jump in your car and start driving without knowing where you're headed, would you?
You'd plan your route, decide on the places you want to visit, make a list of things you want to do.

In a way, setting goals for your life is similar. It's like planning your personal journey, deciding what you want to achieve, and outlining the steps you need to take to get there.

And here's the best part. By setting goals, you're not only giving your future a shape, but you're also strengthening your present. Because when you have clear goals, you be motivated, focus, a sense of purpose. And these are powerful tools that can help you embrace your newfound happiness and independence.

So, let's dive into the journey of goal setting. Let's grab that pen and paper and start envisioning our brighter future. And remember, it's not just about setting goals; it's about believing in them, in you, and in the amazing journey that lies ahead.

Strategies for Effective Goal Setting

Alright, so we've discussed the importance of goal setting in crafting our future. Now let's talk about how to do it effectively. You know, the real, gritty work of it all.

Because let's face it, goal setting is not a walk in the park. It requires thought, effort, and most importantly, a commitment to yourself. But don't worry, I've got your back. Here are some strategies to help you on this exciting journey.

Let's start with specificity. This is a fancy word, but it simply means being precise with what you want. For instance, instead of saying "I want to be fit," try "I want to be able to run a 5k in 30 minutes within the next 3 months." See the difference? The latter goal is clear, specific, and measurable. It's also easier to plan actions around it.

Next, think about why this goal is important to you. This 'why' will be your fuel, your motivator when things get a little tough, because let's be real, they sometimes do. So write down your reasons. Let them serve as reminders of why you started this journey in the first place.

Third, break your goal down into smaller, manageable steps. We're not climbing the mountain in one giant leap, right? So instead of getting overwhelmed by the big picture, focus on the small steps you can take each day.

For example, if your goal is to write a book, start with writing a paragraph or a page each day. The journey of a thousand miles begins with a single step, remember?

And finally, set some deadlines. Now, this might sound a little harsh, but deadlines actually help us stay on track. They give us a sense of urgency and help us prioritize our goals.

Just make sure they're realistic. Setting a goal to become fluent in Spanish in a week isn't just unrealistic, it's setting yourself up for disappointment.

Now, with these strategies in your toolbox, you're all set for your goal-setting journey. And remember, goal setting is not a one-time thing. It's a continuous process. You might have to tweak your goals along the way, and that's perfectly okay.

Life is unpredictable, and so are we. The most important thing is to stay committed to your journey, and always, always believe in yourself. Because you are capable of achieving incredible things.

Staying Motivated and Committed to Your Vision for the Future

Staying motivated can be challenging, especially when the initial excitement of setting a new goal starts to fade, and you're left staring at the mountain of work ahead of you. But here's the thing: motivation is not always a given. It's not something that's just there all the time. Sometimes, you have to create it.

So, how do you do that?

One of the most effective ways is by keeping your vision for the future at the forefront of your mind. Picture it vividly. Imagine how it would feel to achieve your goal, to live that life you're working towards. This is not some magic trick. It's about creating a deep connection with your goals. By doing so, you're more likely to stay committed even when the going gets tough.

Another way to stay motivated is by reminding yourself of your 'why'. Why is this goal important to you? What impact will it have on your life?

These reminders can help reignite your motivation when it starts to wane. They can help you push through those tough moments and keep you committed to your vision.

Also, celebrate your progress along the way. Each step you take towards your goal is a victory, no matter how small. Remember those smaller, manageable steps we talked about earlier? Well, each one deserves a pat on the back. Celebrating these small wins can boost your motivation and make the journey more enjoyable.

And don't forget the power of positive self-talk. The way you talk to yourself matters. If you're constantly telling yourself that you can't do it, that it's too hard, you're likely to lose motivation. But if you encourage yourself, if you remind yourself of your strengths and abilities, you're more likely to stay motivated and committed. Finally, embrace flexibility.

Your goals are important, yes. But it's okay to change them if they no longer align with your vision for the future. Being rigid can lead to frustration and burnout.

Being flexible, on the other hand, can help you stay committed without feeling overwhelmed or stuck. Staying motivated and committed to your vision for the future is a journey in itself. It's not always easy, but it's absolutely possible. And remember, you don't have to do it alone. Reach out to supportive friends, family members, or a mentor who can cheer you on. The key is to keep moving forward, one step at a time. Because every step brings you closer to your vision for the future.

Chapter 10

Eat, Pray, And Love It

"This is a good sign, having a broken heart. It means we have tried for something."

– Elizabeth Gilbert

Everyone who has experienced divorce, or is even contemplating one, can attest that it is not an easy process, and it is not the easy way out. Being divorced may be preferable to staying in an unhappy marriage but it does not make the extraction a humdrum event.

Nevertheless, we are where we are, and we have the opportunity to make the best of it by changing our outlook on life. Divorce can be one of the hardest circumstances anyone can experience and once we find ourselves on the other side, it can feel like a rebirth or a new lease on life.

When you were married, you had to make some concessions and compromises along the way. Most likely, there are things or experiences that you gave up. Perhaps willingly or even unwillingly.

Now that you are on the other side of divorce (or even still in the midst of it but well on your way), you can start to make the best of your brand-new life.

This means that there is a whole new world out there for you to explore. New experiences to try and enjoy. You can start to do the things that you never could while you were married.

Start thinking about these and start making some goals toward achieving or living them. Perhaps it is travelling the world, going back to school to upgrade your education, running a marathon, moving to a new city, starting your own business, or getting a new job.

You can start to write these down and decide which ones you want to do first and prioritize them. Just doing this will energize you and start to give you a positive outlook on life. Below are some ideas to get you started. They are not the be all and end all but something to get your brainstorming started and trigger new ideas.

One of the easiest (or hardest, depending on your view) things you can do is to start purging. This is about designing your living space the way you want and in a manner that brings you the most joy and peace. If there is a remnant of your ex that brings up bad memories or causes turmoil, get rid of it. You can either give it back to them, donate it, sell it, or burn it. Dealer's choice here!

These items can include things like family photos or mementos, so carefully consider what to do with items like these that are not easily replaceable. If you have no wish to keep certain photos or family videos, consider passing them on to your children (if you have any).

These may not mean much to you, but they may be something your children cherish. Remember that you are divorcing your ex, not your ex from your children.

Wedding rings are personal items and can mean different things to different people. They may also have financial value. Have you thought about what to do with your wedding (and engagement) ring?

During my divorce, I was conflicted and didn't feel right removing my wedding ring for many months. Over time, as the reality of the divorce was setting in, I began to feel less and less attached to it.

One day, while I was out exploring the new city I was living in, I found myself crossing a bridge on foot. I stopped somewhere in the middle to observe and take in all the views that were available. In that moment, without premeditated thought, I slipped the ring off my finger, dangled it over the side of the bridge, and watched it sink in the calm waters below. It felt soothing and brought a moment of closure. I felt freedom reign since that day.

That may not be your plan for your wedding ring but just ensure that, whatever you decide to do with it, it feels organic and brings you peace.

You may want to redecorate your living space. Moving things around, changing wall colors, replacing furniture, or repurposing a room, can change your immediate environment to match your new attitude.

My ex and I had bought a condo while we were still together but well on our way to separation. After the separation and my ex moved to another part of the country, I lived in the condo for a few months leaving things as is.

One day, I woke up that morning, and on my way to the kitchen, I realized how depressing the place looked. Is this where I actually live, I thought? No wonder the times felt dark! That day, I scanned around the entire condo and decided it was time to brighten things up.

The first thing I did was remove all the 1970s window coverings. Wow! The sun was actually shining through the windows and the place looked 3 decades more modern. I sat that day, in different spots and in different rooms, envisioning what could be.

I then spent the next 2 months repainting every room, changing almost every piece of furniture, adding décor items, and changing out all the light fixtures. When I was done, it was now my sanctuary.

On the surface, it may seem as though changing your living space is like rearranging the deck chairs on the Titanic. However, you spend a lot of time in your living space. It needs to be warm, inviting, and bring you some kind of solace.

Next up is leisure and travel. Are there places you always wanted to travel to and visit or experiences you always wanted to have but never could?

Now is the time to plan those. It's time to break out of the same old, same old routine and scenery and explore the world. Unlike material objects, experiences open our horizons and create memories we will have for the rest of our lives.

Travelling to exotic new places, experiencing diverse cultures, and learning about rich history helps us to understand that there is a world out there bigger than ourselves. Stand in awe of natural wonders, enjoy local cuisine, take in the thrill of big city lights, or relax in the tranquility of remote areas.

Travelling with family, friends, or even alone, can help break us out of our monotony. It allows us to connect with new people and find adventure in life.

While trying to change your scenery, why not also change your look? Consider updating or upgrading your wardrobe. Is your style falling behind by a couple of decades?

Even if you don't know what style you may want, explore different looks and styles, until you find one that's right for you. Updating your wardrobe can take years off your look and your perceived age.

While you are at it, why not consider a new hairstyle? Get extensions or cut it short. Straighten or curl it. Change to a new color. It's all up to you and that's the best part. You are now empowered to make decisions for yourself that will affect your persona.

The main message is that your divorce is not the beginning of the end. It's a new beginning. Chances are you have many years, even decades ahead of you. This is a chance at a rebirth, at a new life, and a new you.

Eat, pray, and love it!

Conclusion: Embracing Your New Destiny

The journey of a thousand miles begins with one step. But the journey through divorce can often feel like it's a thousand steps, each one heavier than the last. The pain, the fear, the loneliness - they all weigh on your soul. But each step you take is a step towards healing, towards acceptance, and towards your new destiny.

When we began this book, we were in a place of darkness. We were ensnared in the throes of denial, battling the stormy waves of emotional trauma, and straining under the weight of societal judgement. It seemed a Herculean task to rediscover ourselves and build a new life post-divorce. But as we've journeyed through these chapters, we've shed light on the darkness, faced the storm, and began to lift the weight from our shoulders.

Our compass, oriented towards our values and beliefs, keeps us grounded and pointed in the direction of growth. Our sails, filled with the winds of change, propel us forward, despite the challenging seas we may encounter.

As we now stand on the precipice of this new life, we can look back and see the obstacles we've overcome. We can look inward and appreciate the strength and resilience we've discovered. And we can look forward, to the future that awaits us.

That future may still be uncertain. There may still be challenges to face, fears to overcome, and losses to mourn. But we are not the same person who began this journey. We are stronger, wiser, and more resilient. We have let go of the past and embraced the reality of our divorce. We have faced our fears and stepped into the unknown. We have overcome our pain and found healing.

So, as you close this book and open the next chapter of your life, remember this: You are not defined by your divorce. You are defined by the person you've become through it - a person of strength, resilience, and courage. A person capable of facing adversity, learning from it, and growing through it.

Don't look at your divorce as an ending. See it as a new beginning. A fresh start. An opportunity to reinvent yourself and create a life that's true to who you are and what you value.

You have a future to shape, dreams to chase, and a life to live to the fullest. Embrace this opportunity with open arms and an open heart. This is your journey, your story. Make it a story of resilience, growth, and ultimately, of hope.

Remember, your journey does not stop here. It continues every day, with every decision you make, and with every step you take. And just as you've found guidance in this book, I hope you continue to seek wisdom, nurture your spirit, and cultivate inner peace as you move forward.

As Lena Horne said, "It's not the load that breaks you down, it's the way you carry it." Carry your past experiences not as burdens, but as lessons. Carry your pain not as a wound, but as a testament to your strength. Carry your future not as a fear, but as a beacon of hope.

Thank you for taking this journey with me. I hope it has been as transformative for you as it has been for me. If you wish to take the next step of your journey with me, I suggest reading the second book of this series called Alone: What Now?.

It outlines practical steps you can take, such as financial independence, maintaining healthy relationships with your children after divorce, nurturing your physical and mental health, and exploring the world of dating after divorce. Now that you have navigated through the emotional journey, when you are ready, you can now turn your attention to the practical part of your journey.

As you close this book, remember that the process of healing and growth is not a destination, but a journey. It doesn't end here. It continues every day, with every decision you make, and with every step you take. Embrace your new destiny.

The journey to your future starts now.

Printed in Great Britain
by Amazon

36411001R00109